# THE EPIC OF GILGAMESH

*Anonymous - Gilgamesh*

AUTHORED by Amit Dave
UPDATED AND REVISED by Bella Wang

COVER DESIGN by Table XI Partners LLC
COVER PHOTO by Olivia Verma and © 2005 GradeSaver, LLC

BOOK DESIGN by Table XI Partners LLC

Published by GradeSaver LLC, www.gradesaver.com

First published in the United States of America by GradeSaver LLC. 2011

GRADESAVER, the GradeSaver logo and the phrase "Getting you the grade since 1999" are registered trademarks of GradeSaver, LLC

ISBN 978-1-60259-266-7

Printed in the United States of America

For other products and additional information please visit
http://www.gradesaver.com

# Table of Contents

# Table of Contents

# Biography of Anonymous - Gilgamesh (n/a-n/a)

The authors of this epic poem remain largely anonymous. The latest and most complete version ever found was composed no later than around 600 BCE, and was signed by a Babylonian author who called himself Sin-Leqi-Unninni. This is the Akkadian version and is usually the basis of most translations. It is one of the earliest known works of literature.

# About The Epic of Gilgamesh

*The Epic of Gilgamesh* is an ancient epic poem from Mesopotamia dating back to roughly 2000 BCE. It is believed to be one of the earliest works of literature in human history. Scholars believe that its origins were in ancient Sumerian poems that were later collected into an Akkadian epic in the 18th or 17th century BCE. Hormuzd Rassam, an Assyrian archaeologist, first discovered the clay tablets that record the epic in 1853, in modern-day Iraq. They were first translated by George Smith, a British Assyriologist, and were first published in the early 1870s.

Eleven tablets make up the main body of the poem. A twelfth tablet was likely added later, but it is not clear why. The twelfth tablet uses similar imagery and concepts but is not sequential to the other eleven. This last tablet is sometimes omitted from translations for this reason.

About The Epic of Gilgamesh

# Character List

### Gilgamesh

The protagonist of the story and the King of Uruk. He is credited with having built the city walls of Uruk to protect its people. In most translations, he is described as being one-third man and two-thirds god. His mother is Ninsun, a goddess. His father is Lugalbanda, a past King of Uruk.

### Enkidu

A wild man who becomes Gilgamesh's best friend. After being visited by Shamhat, the prostitute, Enkidu is civilized and leaves the animal world behind to journey with Shamhat to Uruk. Enkidu accompanies Gilgamesh to defeat Humbaba before he passes away. Gilgamesh journeys to the Underworld to try to bring Enkidu back to life.

### Shamhat

A temple prostitute sent by Gilgamesh to civilize Enkidu. Shamhat seduces Enkidu and he sleeps with her for six days and seven nights. She brings him back to Uruk with her where he first encounters Gilgamesh.

### Ninsun

Gilgamesh's mother and a goddess. She prays for Gilgamesh and Enkidu before they embark to fight Humbaba in the cedar forest.

### Humbaba/Huwawa

The Guardian of the cedar forest. Humbaba is defeated and killed by Gilgamesh and Enkidu.

### Ishtar/Irnini

Goddess of Love, Fertility, and War, and daughter of Anu. Ishtar sends the Bull of Heaven to attack Gilgamesh after he spurns her advances.

### Anu

The father of the Sumerian Gods. Ishtar appeals to him for help after Gilgamesh spurns her advances.

### Urshanabi

The boatman who takes Gilgamesh over the waters of the dead to see Utnapishtim.

### Utnapishtim

Instructed by Ea to build a boat before the flood that destroyed the city of Shurrupak. Utnapishtim is granted immortality for his role. Gilgamesh seeks him out after Enkidu's death. Utnapishtim tells Gilgamesh of the flood and tells him where to find a magic plant that can grant immortality.

## The Bull of Heaven

Referred to in some translations as "Gugalanna," the Bull of Heaven was sent to punish Gilgamesh for rejecting Ishtar's sexual advances. Gilgamesh and Enkidu slay the Bull of Heaven and insult Ishtar.

## Siduri

A barmaid and alewife that Gilgamesh encounters on his journey into the Underworld. Siduri resides in a cottage by the sea. She discourages Gilgamesh on his pursuit for immortality but ultimately directs him to the boatman Urshanabi.

## Enlil

The storm god, wind god, and god of destiny.

## Lugalbanda

The father of Gilgamesh, a great hero king of Uruk.

## Aruru/Mammetum

The mother goddess who established life and death.

## Nergal

Lord of the underworld.

## Ninurta

The god of war, chaos, and silence.

## Shamash

The god of light and the sun, he aids Enkidu and Gilgamesh in their fight with Humbaba.

## Sin

The god of the moon.

## Sumuqan

The god of cattle.

# Major Themes

### Love and Friendship

When we first meet Gilgamesh, he is a tyrant king who terrifies the people of Uruk. Only after meeting Enkidu and becoming his friend does Gilgamesh transform into a hero worthy of memory. This transformative effect is also exacted on Enkidu, who Gilgamesh helps move beyond his fears. The platonic love the two have for each other helps Gilgamesh become a better leader to his people by allowing him to better understand and identify with them. When considered in tandem with the theme of death in the poem, love and friendship can be viewed not only as a part of life, but as a necessary component to give existence meaning.

### Death

The major theme of the poem is that of mortality. Gilgamesh must learn the difficult lesson that, even as a king, he too must face the reality of his own death. On their way to the Cedar Forst to face Humbaba, Enkidu expresses his concerns about death, which Gilgamesh laughs off, telling Enkidu that no one lives forever and that life is short. However, when Enkidu dies, Gilgamesh is so distraught that he seeks out Utnapishtim to learn the secret of immortality. Despite his hopes, Utnapishtim tells Gilgamesh the story of the flood. He explains to Gilgamesh that the quest for immortality is a futile one, as creation itself also contains the seed of death, making it inescapable. The Gods, he explains, intentionally did this. Gilgamesh returns to Uruk having learned that the quality of one's life is measured not by wealth or fame, but by the quality of the time he spent while alive and the people with which he surrounded himself.

### The Hero's Journey or Quest

A common theme in mythology and ancient stories, Gilgamesh's story is no exception. The hero must embark on a journey or quest in order to discover who he is. Initially, Enkidu travels from the wilderness with Shamhat to civilization to meet Gilgamesh. Gilgamesh begins his quest with Enkidu by traveling to the Cedar Forest to defeat Humbaba. After Enkidu's death, Gilgamesh's personal journey begins. He seeks out Utnapishtim to learn the secret of immortality. His journey concludes with his return to Uruk. In this case, Gilgamesh's journey is a direct reflection of his internal struggle and "journey" to become a better, selfless leader.

### The Wrath of the Gods

Gilgamesh expresses his jealousy towards the gods and the immortality they enjoy. He and Enkidu learn firsthand that incurring the wrath of the gods can have disastrous consequences. Rather than wise, omniscient beings, the gods in Gilgamesh are vengeful and easily angered. Gilgamesh and Enkidu first encounter this wrath after Gilgamesh rejects Ishtar's advances. Ishtar immediately turns to her father, Anu, to send the Bull of Heaven to punish Gilgamesh. At first, Anu rejects Ishtar's request but she threatens to raise the dead to devour the living. Anu is frightened by Ishtar's threat and releases the Bull of Heaven to appease her. When Gilgamesh and Enkidu slay the Bull of Heaven, they further insult Ishtar by throwing the Bull's hindquarters at her face. Enkidu later dreams that the gods have decided that he must die for these transgressions. After twelve days of suffering, he dies a painful death.

Utnapishtim also tells Gilgamesh the story of a great flood exacted on the people of Shurrupak. Ea informs Utnapishtim of the coming flood and instructs him to build a great boat and to stock that boat with all the creatures of the land. It is important to note that when Utnapishtim asks Ea about why the flood is coming and about what he should tell the people of Shurrupak, Ea has no specific answer for him, stating only that Enlil is angry. This suggests that the wrath of the gods can also be incurred without any obvious insult or explanation.

## Gateways

Gateways and doors by their very nature symbolize separation, but also transition. Although a physical doorway is not present in the beginning, Enkidu must transition from the wilderness to civilization. In this sense, Shamhat herself represents a gateway. Enkidu then enters Uruk with Shamhat, passing through the city's great walls. Enkidu and Gilgamesh later discuss Enkidu's fear at the gate to the Cedar Forest. They cut down the tallest tree in the forest to make into a gate for Uruk. On his journey to find Utnapishtim, Gilgamesh must pass through the gate of Mashu, guarded by the Scorpion men. At each point when a gateway is encountered, a decision must be made by Gilgamesh or Enkidu as to whether they will continue or turn back. Utilized in this manner, gateways also serve as an effective literary device to force characters to make decisions that affect the overall narrative.

## Baptism or Ritual Cleansing

Water is continually used by characters in Gilgamesh at key points in the story to wash themselves but also marks an important point of transition. In this way, water is used in a baptismal manner. Enkidu washes himself after meeting Shamhat, marking his transition from the wilderness to civilization. Gilgamesh and Enkidu wash themselves after slaying the Bull of Heaven. Gilgamesh bathes himself after acquiring the magic plant to achieve immortality. In each case, a ritual cleansing marks an important moment in the story. Enkidu is transformed, leaving behind the world of animals and nature and entering the world of humans. Gilgamesh loses the magic plant but transitions to accepting his mortality.

## Responsibility

Gilgamesh is introduced to us as a tyrant king who does as he pleases and has little regard for his subjects. Aruru creates Enkidu to strike a balance against

Gilgamesh's tyrannical ways. His purpose in the story is to help Gilgamesh become the king he needs to be and to teach him about what is most valuable in life. Through this ordeal, Gilgamesh loses his best friend and must face reality. The recklessness with which he previously had lived his life is evidently unsustainable. Gilgamesh learns that just as he will not live forever, he will age, and with that age must come maturity and wisdom if he is to live a life worth living.

# Glossary of Terms

**Akkadian**

A Semitic language, it is the source language for most versions of Gilgamesh read today.

**Apsu**

The great abyss of waters beneath the earth.

**Bitumen**

A thick tarlike substance used for waterproofing and as an adhesive.

**Carnelian**

A semi-precious reddish-brown mineral used for gemstones.

**Cedar Forest**

A sacred forest, home of Humbaba/Huwawa, who is its guardian.

**Cuneiform**

Meaning "wedge-shaped," it is the script used to record languages such as Sumerian and Akkadian. Cuneiform was written by pressing a reed stylus into a clay tablet.

**Euphrates River**

One of the two great rivers of Mesopotamia, the other being the Tigris. Uruk is situated upon the Euphrates.

**Harlot**

A priestess or servant in the Temple of Ishtar. Shamhat is one of these prostitutes.

**How-the-Old-Man-Once-Again-Becomes-A-Young-Man**

A magic plant that Utnapishtim tells Gilgamesh can restore one's youth. Utnapishtim tells Gilgamesh that the plant can be found at the bottom of the sea.

**King Ashurbanipal**

An Assyrian king who was the last great king of the Neo-Assyrian Empire. His court library, excavated at Nineveh, contained a good deal of Mesopotamian literature, including the tablets on which the Epic of Gilgamesh was inscribed.

**Lapis lazuli**

A semi-precious stone prized for its deep blue color. It is mentioned several times in the story, most notably because Gilgamesh's story is said to be recorded on tablets made of it.

**League**

A unit of measurement equal to about a mile and a half.

**Mashu**

A mountain with twin peaks at the edge of the underworld. The sun is said to rise at the eastern peak and make its way down through the western peak.

**Nisir**

The name of the mountain where Utnapishtim's boat came to land.

**Priest-king**

Gilgamesh is the priest-king of Uruk, the spiritual and political leader of the city.

**Seven Sages**

Said to have laid the foundation of Uruk, they were instructed in the arts of civilization by the gods who gave them the plans for the city.

**Shuruppak**

An ancient city destroyed by the Flood during the leadership of Utnapishtim.

**Sin-Leqi-Unninni**

Possibly a priest, he is believed to have lived in Uruk during the Middle Babylonian period. He appears to have produced the most recent version of the epic that is read today.

**The Flood**

An event that was already ancient by Gilgamesh's time, the Flood was brought by the gods for unclear reasons against the city of Shurrupak, thereby destroying all living things.

**Uruk**

*Erech* in the Bible, Uruk was the great walled city ruled by Gilgamesh.

**Ziggurat**

A stepped tower atop which sacrifices were made to appease the gods.

# Short Summary

Gilgamesh is the Priest-King of the city of Uruk. He is a tyrannical king who works his people to death and takes what he wants from them. He kills the young men at will and uses the women as he pleases. The people of Uruk cry out to the gods for help so that they can have peace.

The gods hear them and instruct Anu, the goddess of creation, to make a twin for Gilgamesh, someone who is strong enough to stand up to him and who will ultimately save him. Anu makes Enkidu, a hairy wild man who lives in the wilderness with the animals.

One day a trapper sees Enkidu by a water hole and is frightened. He tells his father of the wild man he saw. His father tells the trapper to go to see Gilgamesh. He tells his son to ask the king for a temple prostitute to bring back with him to seduce Enkidu. The trapper returns with Shamhat, a temple prostitute from the temple of Ishtar, the goddess of love and war. They wait for Enkidu to reappear by the watering hole.

Enkidu returns and Shamhat reveals herself to him. They copulate for six days and seven nights. When Enkidu is satisfied, he finds that the animals no longer accept him. Shamhat tells him to come back with her to Uruk. Upon hearing of Gilgamesh, Enkidu decides he wishes to meet him. The two set out for Uruk, making a stop at a shepherd's camp. There Enkidu learns that Gilgamesh will sleep with a newly married bride on her wedding night, before her husband sleeps with her. He is outraged and decides he must stop Gilgamesh. Meanwhile, Gilgamesh has several dreams foretelling the arrival of Enkidu.

The two meet in the streets of Uruk and a great fight breaks out between them. Gilgamesh is triumphant but his encounter with Enkidu changes him. They become companions. Enkidu tells Gilgamesh of Humbaba, a terrible monster who guards the Cedar Forest. Gilgamesh decides the two of them should journey there and defeat the monster.

They make preparations and head to the Cedar Forest. They encounter Humbaba and with the help of Shamash, the sun god, defeat him. They return to Uruk carrying his head. After a celebration, Gilgamesh bathes himself and catches the eye of Ishtar. She tells him to become her lover, promising great riches and rewards in return. Gilgamesh rejects Ishtar, telling her he is aware of her reputation as a scornful lover.

Ishtar is outraged and convinces her father, Anu, to release the Bull of Heaven to punish Gilgamesh. The Bull of Heaven descends on Uruk, killing hundreds of men. Enkidu seizes the animal and Gilgamesh kills it with a sword. Ishtar appears and threatens the heroes. Enkidu tears off one of the Bull's haunches and throws it at Ishtar. Later that night, Enkidu has a dream that the gods are meeting in council.

The dream proves true. The gods decide that one of the heroes must die for their behavior. They choose Enkidu. Enkidu falls ill and suffers for twelve days before finally dying. Gilgamesh is shattered. He mourns for days and tears his hair and clothes. He adorns filthy animal skins and journeys into the forest and mountains. He has witnessed death and is now terrified of his own mortality. He seeks to escape it.

Gilgamesh decides to seek out Utnapishtim, the one being granted immortality by the gods. He travels to Mount Mashu, a twin-peaked mountain that marks an entrance to a world in which mortals cannot venture. He convinces the guards of the mountain, two Scorpion-man beings, to allow him to enter a long passage under the mountain. He endures this terrible darkness for a full day.

When he emerges on the other side, he is in a wondrous paradise. He sees a tavern by the sea and approaches it, frightening its owner, Siduri, with his appearance. Siduri allows him to enter the tavern after he explains his story and his intention to find Utnapishtim. Siduri tells Gilgamesh of Urshanabi, the boatman, who can ferry Gilgamesh across the Waters of Death to where Utnapishtim resides.

Gilgamesh finds Urshanabi and the two set out to find Utnapishtim. They reach a shore and Gilgamesh meets an old man. Gilgamesh explains that he wishes to attain immortality. The old man is Utnapishtim, who tells Gilgamesh that immortality is for the gods alone. Mortals must learn to accept death. He tells Gilgamesh the story of how he was granted immortality by the gods. He asks Gilgamesh what he has done to deserve this same gift.

Gilgamesh finally leaves with Urshanabi to return to Uruk. Utnapishtim tells Gilgamesh of a magical plant at the bottom of the sea that can restore one's youth. Gilgamesh descends into the waters and retrieves the plant.

On his way back to Uruk, Gilgamesh stops to bathe in a spring, leaving the plant by the water. A serpent appears and steals the plant, leaving Gilgamesh weeping by the water's edge. He returns to Uruk with Urshanabi. Upon seeing the great city, Gilgamesh understands that it is his legacy, and that if he rules well, it will be his greatest legacy. Gilgamesh comes to understand that the most important thing in life is to have lived and loved well.

# Quotes and Analysis

"For seven days Enkidu in his wonder

Lay with her in pleasure, and then at last
went to seek out the company of the creatures

whose hearts delight in feeding upon the grasslands,
and visiting the watering places, and

ranging the hills. But seeing him, they fled.
The creatures were gone, and everything was changed.

His body that loved to range the hills was now
unable to follow; but in the mind of the wild man

there was beginning a new understanding.
Bewildered, he turned, and sought out the company

of the temple prostitute.

*Ferry, p. 8-9*

Following his encounter with Shamhat, Enkidu is introduced to sexuality and this becomes a civilizing force. He is now a human being who has become self-aware. The animals who were his friends realize the change in him and abandon him. He is no longer able to roam the plains with the same energy he did before. Through sexuality Enkidu comes to gain a new self-understanding, which initially frightens him. He seeks assistance from Shamhat to reconcile these new thoughts.

"But Enkidu knew nothing about these things,
so he sat and stared at the cooked food and the beer

for a very long time, not knowing what to do.
Then Shamhat, the harlot, the temple prostitute,

said: 'Enkidu, this is the food and drink
men eat and drink. Eat and drink your fill.'

So Enkidu ate his fill of the cooked food,
and drank the beer. Seven jugs of the beer

and he was suddenly joyful, and sang aloud.
Then he washed his hairy body, anointed himself

with oil, and dressed his body in new clothes,
so that he looked as beautiful as a bridegroom.

He took up a weapon to guard the flocks and shepherds
against the wolves and lions that preyed upon them.

Therefore, at night, with Enkidu to guard them,
the shepherds could lie down in peaceful sleep."

*Ferry, p. 12-13*

This passage demonstrates Enkidu's initial innocence in the ways of humans, but
ends with his transformation. Once again, Shamhat shepherds him through this
transformation as Enkidu imbibes alcohol for the first time and then washes and
dresses himself in fine clothing. Most notable is that Enkidu then takes up watch to
protect the shepherds from the animals of the natural world of which he was once a
member. This marks his transition from an animal to a man who now guards against
the intrusion of nature.

"Where is the strength? It is Gilgamesh
who will venture first into the Cedar Forest,

and you can follow after, crying out:
'Go on, go forward, go on, embrace the danger!'

You who have fought with lions and with wolves,
you know what danger is. Where is your courage?

If I should fall, my name will be secure.
'It was Gilgamesh who fought against Huwawa!

It is Gilgamesh who will venture into the Forest
and cut down the Cedar down and win the glory.

My fame will be secure to all my sons.'"

*Ferry, p. 17*

Here, Gilgamesh admonishes Enkidu's fear prior to their battle with Humbaba/Huwawa. Gilgamesh boasts of how, regardless of how the battle goes, his fame is cemented. This passage demonstrates Gilgamesh's view of himself and life in general. To him, fame and a legacy are the most important aspects of life. While one can argue that Gilgamesh is only saying these things to encourage Enkidu, he is also clearly on a power trip. Contrast this with how Gilgamesh feels following Enkidu's death.

Gilgamesh answered and said : "What could I offer

the queen of love in return, who lacks nothing at all?
Balm for the body? The food and drink of the gods?

I have nothing to give to her who lacks nothing at all.
You are the door through which the cold gets in.

You are the fire that goes out. You are the pitch
that sticks to the hands of the one who carries the bucket.

You are the house that falls down. You are the shoe
that pinches the foot of the wearer. The ill-made wall

that buckles when time has gone by. The leaky
water skin soaking the water skin carrier."

*Ferry, p. 30*

Following his return to Uruk after defeating Humbaba with Enkidu, Gilgamesh bathes and adorns himself, drawing Ishtar's lustful eye. She asks him to become her lover and promises him riches. Gilgamesh spurns her advances and insults her using artful analogies to suggest that Ishtar is old and undesirable. In other words, Gilgamesh tells the goddess of love that there is nothing attractive or appealing about her, essentially calling her a fraud.

"After the Scorpion Dragon Being spoke,
Gilgamesh went to the entrance into the mountain

and entered the darkness alone, without a companion.
By the time he reached the end of the first league

the darkness was total, nothing behind or before.
He made his way, companionless, to the end

of the second league. Utterly lightless, black.
There was nothing behind or before, nothing at all.

Only, the blackness pressed in upon his body.
He felt his blind way through the mountain tunnel,

struggling for breath, through the third league, alone,
and companionless through the fourth, making his way,

and struggling for every breath, to the end of the fifth,
in the absolute dark, nothing behind or before,

the weight of the blackness pressing in upon him."

*Ferry, p. 51*

After entering into the mountain passage beneath Mount Mashu, Gilgamesh enters
complete darkness and struggles to find his way. This ordeal tests him as he totally
and completely alone and now has to face his loneliness and his inner thoughts.
Darkness generally represents the unknown and we tend to project our fears onto the
unknown. In this environment, there is no solace for Gilgamesh and no means of
escape; once he enters the only way out is the way through. It is necessary for his
transformation and for his salvation.

"Seven days and nights I sat beside the body,
weeping for Enkidu beside the body,

and then I saw a worm fall out of his nose.
Must I die too? Must Gilgamesh be like that?

It was then I felt the fear of it in my belly.
I roam the wilderness because of the fear.

Enkidu, the companion, whom I loved,
is dirt, nothing but clay is Enkidu.

Weeping as if I were a woman I roam
the paths and shores of unknown places saying:

'Must I die too? Must Gilgamesh be like that?'"

Here, Gilgamesh tells the story of his predicament to Siduri, the tavern-keeper. Having witnessed the death of his close friend, Gilgamesh is overcome with the fear of his own death and seeks desperately to escape his fate. The repetition of the line, "Must I die too? Must Gilgamesh be like that?" suggests that Gilgamesh perceives himself as somehow exempt from mortality. Given how he has lived his life up to this point, taking what he wants when he wants, the sudden realization that it will all end is more than he can bear. Despite all his fame and his accomplishments, he cannot take it with him.

"Who is the mortal who can live forever?
The life of man is short. Only the gods

can live forever. Therefore put on new clothes,
a clean robe and a cloak tied with a sash,

and wash the filth of the journey from your body.
Eat and drink your fill of the food and drink

men eat and drink. Let there be pleasure and dancing."

Siduri implores Gilgamesh to abandon his quest and partake in the joys of life instead, explaining that immortality was never designed for mortal men. She advises him to make the most of what he has, a life that is still in progress, and to enjoy each moment instead of pining for what he cannot have.

"Utnapishtim, son of Ubartutu,
abandon your house, abandon what you possess.

abandon your house and build a boat instead.
Seek life instead of riches, save yourself.

Take with you, on the boat you build, an instance
of each thing living so that they may be

safe from obliteration in the flood.
Perform the construction of the boat with care.

Let the length of the boat and the width of the boat be equal.
Roof over the boat as the abyss is roofed."

*Ferry, p. 66*

Here, Ea instructs Utnapishtim to build an ark in anticipation of the flood to come. Its similarity to the Bible story of Noah is apparent. Utnapishtim's instructions are nearly identical to those of Noah. Most important is Ea's emphasis of seeking life instead of riches. While Ea is speaking of saving all the life in Shuruppak, this line is also an important theme in the epic overall. Gilgamesh learns to seek a life of quality rather than quantity; a life of companionship and love, not a life of fame and fortune.

Gilgamesh said to Urshanabi the boatman:
"Urshanabi, this plant is a wonderful plant.

New life may be obtained by means of it.
I will carry the thorny plant back to my city.

I will give some of the plant to the elders there,
to share among them, telling them it is called

How-the-Old-Man-Once-Again-Becomes-A-Young-Man.
And I will take my share of the magic plant,

once more to become the one who is youngest and strongest."

*Ferry, p. 80*

Gilgamesh shares his plan with Urshanabi. He wishes to take the plant back to Uruk and test it on the elders to see if its powers hold true. If so, he too would partake and reclaim his youth, and his reputation, thereby remaining the strongest and youngest in Uruk. Gilgamesh's enthusiasm for the plan demonstrates the folly of youth and the regret of age. As we age, we tend to wish we still had our youth to put that energy to better use. This passage is reminiscent of the adage, "Youth is wasted on the young."

At twenty leagues they stopped only to eat.
At thirty leagues they stopped to rest for the night.

And so they traveled until they reached Uruk.
There Gilgamesh the king said to the boatman:

"Study the brickwork, study the fortification;
climb the ancient staircase to the terrace;

study how it is made; from the terrace see
the planted and fallow fields, the ponds and orchards.

One league is the inner city, another league
is orchards; still another the fields beyond;

over there is the precinct of the temple. . . ,
Three leagues and the temple precinct of Ishtar

Measure Uruk, the city of Gilgamesh."

*Ferry, p. 81-82*

This passage marks Gilgamesh's return to Uruk with Urshanabi, the boatman, at his side. It marks his acceptance of his mortality, as he now sees Uruk with new appreciation. Here, he details the city's features to Urshanabi, echoing the lines that mark the beginning of the story. This is of importance not only because it demonstrates that Gilgamesh has a new understanding of life, but that we too, as the readers, can understand Gilgamesh's state of mind simply by the repetition of these lines. Rather than telling us directly how Gilgamesh feels, this passage shows us that his transformation is complete.

# Summary and Analysis of Tablet I

## Summary

The story begins with a prologue introducing us to the main character, Gilgamesh, the Priest-King of Uruk. Gilgamesh's mother is Ninsun, sometimes referred to as the Lady Wildcow Ninsun. She was a goddess, endowing Gilgamesh with a semi-divine nature. Lugulbanda, a priest, was his father. Gilgamesh constructed the great city of Uruk along the Euphrates River in Mesopotamia, and surrounded it intricately decorated walls. He also built a temple for the goddess Ishtar, the goddess of love, and her father Anu, the father of the gods. Gilgamesh is credited with opening passages through the mountains. He traveled to the Nether World and beyond it, where he met Utnapishtim, the sole survivor of the great flood that almost ended the world, the one who had been given immortality. When he returned to Uruk, he wrote everything down on a tablet of lapis lazuli and locked it in a copper chest.

As the story begins, Gilgamesh is a tyrannical leader who shows little regard for his people. He takes what he wants from them and works them to death constructing the walls of Uruk. He sleeps with brides on their wedding night, before their husbands. It is said that no one can resist his power. The old men of Uruk complain and appeal to the gods for help. The gods hear their cries and instruct Aruru, the goddess of creation, to make someone strong enough to act as a counterforce to Gilgamesh.

Aruru takes some clay, moistens it with her spit, and forms another man, named Enkidu. Enkidu resides in the wilderness with the animals, knowing nothing of the civilized world. He lives as one of the animals, running with them and eating what they eat. One day a trapper sees Enkidu at a watering hole. His appearance is frightening as he is huge and covered in hair. The trapper suspects that Enkidu is the one who has been un-setting his traps and filling the pits he uses to catch animals. The trapper returns home and tells his father he has seen a frightening wild man.

The trapper's father advises him to go to Uruk and ask Gilgamesh to lend him a prostitute from the temple of Ishtar to tame Enkidu. After doing so, the trapper returns with Shamhat, the prostitute, and they wait by the watering hole for three days.

When Enkidu does appear again, the trapper tells Shamhat to lie down on a blanket and show Enkidu her breasts and her body. Enkidu is enchanted by Shamhat and lies upon her and they copulate for six days and seven nights. After Enkidu is finally satisfied, he leaves Shamhat and attempts to returns to the animals, but they no longer regard him as one of them and run away from him.

Enkidu finds he has become weaker and can no longer run with the animals as he did before. His mind has been awakened. Troubled by this new self-awareness, he asks Shamhat for help. She tells him about life in Uruk and its king, Gilgamesh. As

Enkidu hears more about Gilgamesh from Shamhat, he begins to feel a need for a companion and decides he wants to meet Gilgamesh.

Meanwhile, Gilgamesh has two dreams that trouble him. In the first dream, a meteor lands in a field outside Uruk. Gilgamesh is drawn to the rock "as if it were a woman." After lifting it, he carries it to his mother, Ninsun. In the second dream, Gilgamesh finds an axe lying in the street. A crowd of people stands around it, admiring it. Gilgamesh is also drawn to the axe, as if it were his wife. He carries it to his mother and lays it at her feet. He tells Ninsun of these dreams. She interprets them to mean that he will soon meet a man, a man who will become his friend and greatest companion.

## Analysis

The narrator introduces Gilgamesh in the past tense—the high walls of the city he built are already ancient. At the same time, he suggests that the story is in Gilgamesh's own words, and that the legendary king himself wrote it down. Gilgamesh's story commemorates historical people and deeds, and at the same time, Gilgamesh's passage through heroism, grief, and wisdom is a perpetual, universal process. The story of Gilgamesh is both timeless and immediate.

Though Gilgamesh's mother Ninsun plays a significant role in the early parts of the story, we learn very little about his father. The Sin-Leqi-Unninni version of Gilgamesh says his father is Ninsun's husband, Lugulbanda, but it is not clear if Lugulbanda is actually Gilgamesh's biological father. Some versions of the poem declare that Gilgamesh's father is a priest, while others call him a "fool." Like Gilgamesh, Lugulbanda was a genuine historical figure. He precedes Gilgamesh on Uruk's king list by two, and he would have more likely been his grandfather, considering the lengths of the recorded reigns. Like Gilgamesh, people worshipped him as a god after his death.

Although Gilgamesh is a king and his story has become legend, the author also includes examples of Gilgamesh's tyrannical behavior. He has no equal, and no one can stand up to him. Gilgamesh's lineage establishes him as one-third mortal and two-thirds a god. Therefore, it is appropriate that the people of Uruk appeal to the gods for help.

Enkidu is described as terrifying in appearance, covered in hair and living with the animals. He is also huge and very strong, characteristics that otherwise are only attributed to Gilgamesh. Enkidu is the untamed wild itself. As Gilgamesh represents civilization and the dominion of man over all, Enkidu is the natural counterweight. It is also notable that despite his great strength, Enkidu is helpless in the face of a woman's sexuality. Shamhat's power civilizes and tames Enkidu to prepare him for his journey to Uruk and ultimately to Gilgamesh. This speaks to a different view of a prostitute in Gilgamesh's time. Rather than being seen as a criminal act, Shamhat's role is revered, even sacred. It is possible that a woman's sexuality was seen as a necessity to tame a man and make him suitable for civilized life, supporting a family, or raising children. Shamhat's taming of Enkidu also foreshadows Enkidu's role in taming Gilgamesh. Shamhat awakens Enkidu. Similarly, Enkidu must awaken Gilgamesh.

Many scholars have seen Biblical parallels in the Epic of Gilgamesh. Enkidu has been compared to Esau and Ishmael, who both exhibited animal-like characteristics, but his story also reflects the civilizing of humankind. As a species, we have moved from a more primal, animal-like existence to one of culture. We educate ourselves and gain insight into our world and ourselves. The biblical motif of Adam and Eve also mirrors Enkidu's story. Their fall from innocence is a result of becoming aware of their sexuality. After that, they are cast out of Eden and must find their own way in the world, just as Enkidu does.

Though sexuality is presented as an important transformational force, the theme of platonic friendship and love ultimately is the more profound one in the story. Some scholars have seen homoerotic qualities in Gilgamesh and Enkidu's relationship, and others feel there is no direct evidence of this in the text. Their relationship is based on a very close friendship and it is this type of relationship that the story presents as the most vital. Enkidu and Gilgamesh balance each other and help each other find inner harmony.

# Summary and Analysis of Tablet II and Tablet III

## Summary

Shamhat divides her robes and uses them to clothe Enkidu. These are the first clothes he has ever worn. She leads him by hand, as if he was a child, and they begin their journey. On their way to Uruk, they stop at a shepherd's camp, where the herdsmen are astonished by Enkidu's size, strength, and beauty. They serve him plates of cooked food, and jugs filled with beer. Enkidu does not even recognize these items as food. Until now, he has eaten only grass and sucked the milk of wild animals. Shamhat encourages him to eat and drink. He drinks seven jugs of beer, and begins singing and dancing. He bathes and anoints himself with oil and dresses in fine new clothes. Shamhat shaves the hair from his body. Enkidu then offers to stand guard over the shepherds and their flocks, protecting them from the wolves and lions that normally threaten their safety.

One day a stranger comes into the camp carrying a highly decorated platter. Enkidu asks Shamhat to find out who he is and where he is going. The man tells them that he is going to a wedding ceremony in Uruk. Gilgamesh will be there and as the King, he will sleep with the bride before her husband does. Whatever Gilgamesh desires, the man explains, he takes—no one can withstand his power. Enkidu finds this to be unacceptable and decides to go to Uruk to challenge Gilgamesh, because he feels sure that he can defeat him. When he arrives in Uruk, the people of the city are amazed to see a man who is as strong and powerful in appearance as Gilgamesh. They crowd around him and hail him as their champion and savior. Enkidu stands on the threshold of the bride's bedchamber and blocks Gilgamesh's path.

The two men begin to wrestle in the street, and the city shakes as they do so. Gilgamesh eventually wrestles Enkidu to the ground and is victorious. Enkidu concedes his defeat and says that Gilgamesh is the rightful king of Uruk. Ninsun tells Gilgamesh that Enkidu has no family, that he has lived his whole life on the plains with the animals. She tells Gilgamesh that Enkidu is loyal and will not abandon his side. Both men forget their anger and declare their loyalty to each other. They kiss and embrace.

Shortly after, the two friends begin looking for a challenge to take on together. Enkidu tells Gilgamesh about a monster named Humbaba, sometimes called Huwawa. He is the guardian of the Cedar Forest, a place forbidden to mortals. Humbaba serves Enlil, who made Humbaba a terrible being whose mouth is fire, his roar is the floodwater, and his breath is death. Gilgamesh is intrigued by this creature and decides that he and Enkidu should meet Humbaba in battle.

Enkidu is frightened at first, telling Gilgamesh that Humbaba cannot be beaten. Gilgamesh dismisses Enkidu's concerns, saying he has no fear of death, so long as he is able to gain fame. The two heroes go to the armor makers of Uruk and obtain axes and swords for the battle. Gilgamesh tells Enkidu that they can both cement their fame by defeating Humbaba.

The elders of Uruk echo Enkidu's concerns. They advise Gilgamesh to let Enkidu lead the way, as Enkidu has knowledge of the wilderness. They also advise Gilgamesh to make an offering to Shamash before embarking. Enkidu tells Gilgamesh that he has his loyalty and that he will lead Gilgamesh through the wilderness to the Cedar Forest.

Upon hearing of Gilgamesh's plans, Ninsun is distraught. She weeps and fears for her son's life. She bathes and dons robes before ascending to the ziggurat, where she makes an offering to Shamash as well. Ninsun prays to Shamash to help and protect Gilgamesh. Finally, she places a sacred pendant around Enkidu's neck and adopts Enkidu as her own son.

## Analysis

Please note that of the majority of Tablet II is missing in the Sin-Leqi-Unninni version, so translators have had to fill in the blanks with older versions of the story.

Enkidu's transformation continues in this tablet as Shamhat clothes him, giving him the first garments he has ever worn. She introduces him to cooked food and to alcohol, uniquely human creations. Enkidu sings and dances after becoming drunk, also something that only humans do. That these events take place at a shepherd's camp is not without relevance. The shepherd's camp is the first sign of civilization that Shamhat and Enkidu encounter on their way to Uruk. As Enkidu is drawn physically closer to Uruk, he is increasingly civilized. The shepherd's camp represents a sort of hybrid of the city and the wilderness. It is neither a city, nor the forest or the plains, but it embodies elements of both. Enkidu takes up weapons to protect the shepherds from the wild animals around them. This action demonstrates his new allegiance to humanity. He has turned away from the natural world he was once a part of it and now greets it with hostility and the threat of violence.

Enkidu is outraged when he hears about how Gilgamesh will sleep with a newly married woman on her wedding night, before her husband does. Despite having no knowledge of the human custom of marriage, Enkidu's sense of justice becomes apparent. He sees Gilgamesh's behavior as fundamentally wrong and immediately decides that he must be the one to right it.

The two giant men wrestle in the streets of Uruk, shaking the city. Though Gilgamesh wins the fight, he is changed because of it. He sees Enkidu not as an opponent but as a worthy companion. Essentially Enkidu tames him, just as Shamhat tamed Enkidu. This idea feeds theories among some scholars that Enkidu and Gilgamesh have more than a platonic relationship. Regardless, Gilgamesh, bolstered by the presence of his new friend, decides he wishes to move beyond Uruk and make his mark on the world.

Humbaba, or Huwawa in some translations, is a vague but terrifying enemy, presented differently depending on the translation. Most translations present him as a terrible monster who personifies evil. Enkidu describes him as a force of nature itself, with a "mouth of fire". Some scholars feel that Humbaba is a personification of an erupting volcano. Volcanoes may have been active in the Mesopotamia region during Gilgamesh's time. The cedar trees guarded by Humbaba would have been very valuable in the relatively treeless region of Mesopotamia where Uruk is located. In any case, Humbaba is something to be feared, a creature of great strength. Despite concerns on the part of the Elders as well as Enkidu's own warnings, Gilgamesh decides he wants to meet Humbaba in battle. He explains that death is not something he fears, as long as he is able to leave behind his mark on the world. This is a markedly different attitude towards death that will change over the course of the poem. Death becomes the predominant theme in the story from here onward.

Although Enkidu's civilization is now complete, the Elders still recognize his wild roots. They see that Enkidu still has knowledge of that world that Gilgamesh does not. Enkidu remains true to his word and tells Gilgamesh that he will not forsake him but will lead him into the wilderness, towards Humbaba. Tablet III ends with Enkidu's adoption by Ninsun, which makes him and Gilgamesh brothers. Ninsun prays for their safe return. This gesture demonstrates that Enkidu's appeal extends to all those he has met in Uruk, not just Gilgamesh. Though they are not blood relatives, they appear as if they are twins. Enkidu's adoption allows him to have a family, a human family that accepts him. When Gilgamesh first met Enkidu, he had no one "to cut his hair." Now, he has a brother whom he will follow into the most dangerous battles.

Summary and Analysis of Tablet II and Tablet III

# Summary and Analysis of Tablet IV and Tablet V

## Summary

The two men, now heavily armed, step outside the seven-bolt gate of Uruk and set off for the Cedar Forest. They do not stop to eat until they have walked twenty leagues. In three days, they cover a distance it would take an ordinary man three weeks to cover. They dig a well and make an offering to the god Shamash, then continue on their journey. As they walk, they encourage one another to offset the fear that begins to grow in them. Each doubts their ability to defeat Humbaba, and in each case, the other reassures them that they will be victorious.

The two heroes stand before the forest's gate, and they see that Humbaba's footsteps have cut clear paths through the woods, indicating his size and might. That night Gilgamesh makes another offering to Shamash the sun god. He prays that Shamash will visit him in a dream and grant him a favorable omen. Gilgamesh and Enkidu construct a shelter against the wind and, huddling together for warmth, lie down, and sleep. At midnight, Gilgamesh wakes from a dream and asks if Enkidu called out to him.

Gilgamesh details the dream to Enkidu: They were walking through a valley when a huge mountain fell on top of them. Enkidu interprets the dream and says that the mountain is Humbaba, and that he and Gilgamesh will topple Humbaba and his dead body will lie like a mountain. The two companions continue their journey through the forest.

After a few days, Gilgamesh makes another offering to Shamash. After falling asleep together, Gilgamesh wakes up again from another dream. He is frightened and asks Enkidu if he touched him. Then he tells Enkidu about this latest dream. In it, Gilgamesh is attacked by a wild bull and pinned to the ground. He is completely trapped when suddenly someone offers him water. Again, Enkidu interprets the dream as fortunate. He says that the bull is not Humbaba, but Shamash, who has blessed Gilgamesh by fighting with him. The one who brought water, Enkidu says, is Gilgamesh's father, Lugulbanda.

As they continue their travels, Gilgamesh makes yet another offering to Shamash and has a third dream. This time he dreams that the earth is shaking and fire and ashes fall from the sky. Gilgamesh tells Enkidu they should reconsider this quest. Once again, Enkidu says the dream is fortunate. Even so, Gilgamesh is filled with fear and doubt. He prays to Shamash again, asking for his protection. Shamash answers and explains that Humbaba has seven garments, each of which spreads terror. Shamash tells Gilgamesh that Humbaba is wearing only one of them now, but warns him that if Humbaba wears all seven, Gilgamesh will be unable to defeat him. The heroes must hurry.

The companions reach the Cedar Forest and begin to chop down trees. Upon doing so they can hear Humbaba roaring. The noise of weapons clashing surrounds them, and Gilgamesh and Enkidu are terrified. They call to each other, reminding each other to be strong and to remember that they can prevail against any odds because of their companionship.

In the heat of the battle, Gilgamesh pleads for help from Shamash. Shamash hears him and unleashes thirteen storms against Humbaba. Humbaba is subdued by this divine onslaught, and Gilgamesh is able to overtake him. Humbaba pleads for mercy and says he knows Gilgamesh is Ninsun's son. He pledges to become his servant if Gilgamesh will only spare his life. Gilgamesh considers this, but Enkidu shouts out and tells Gilgamesh to kill Humbaba quickly.

Humbaba curses Enkidu for this. He suggests that Enkidu is jealous and fearful that Humbaba will supplant him in Gilgamesh's affections. Humbaba reminds them that he is the servant of Enlil, the god of earth, wind, and air—a greater divinity by far than Shamash. If Gilgamesh kills him, he will bring a curse down upon himself. Enkidu ignores these warnings and tells Gilgamesh to hurry up and kill Humbaba before Enlil finds out what they are up to and tries to stop them. Only by killing Humbaba and stealing his cedars can they guarantee their fame. Thus, Humbaba dies.

Gilgamesh cuts down the tallest tree in the forest and uses it to build a new gate for Uruk as a testament to their great adventure. The companions cut down more trees and make a raft, which they use to return to Uruk. On the raft, they carry the gate and the head of Humbaba.

**Analysis**

The extent of Shamash's importance and influence is a major factor in this tablet. Shamash is the sun god, associated with light and wisdom. Humbaba is associated with darkness and evil. Gilgamesh and Enkidu do not seek only to glorify their own names. In seeking to kill Humbaba, Gilgamesh and Enkidu are doing a god's work, even if it will anger another god.

It is remarkable that little detail is provided regarding Gilgamesh and Enkidu's battle with Humbaba. The heroes arrive with weapons forged by artisans in Uruk, but there is little mention of how they are used in the fight. Instead, the narrative focuses more on the fear and terror both characters feel in the face of Humbaba. This may be because little of tablets IV and V exist in the Sin-Leqi-Unnini edition.

Besides evil and darkness, Humbaba also seems to embody fear and the unknown. Enkidu tells Gilgamesh about Humbaba before they arrive at the gate to the Cedar Forest, offering up a truly monstrous description. Before they engage him in battle, Humbaba can be heard roaring in the forest. Huge paths of forest have been cleared by his presence. There is evidence of his size and strength all around them. This is reminiscent of a seldom-seen monster in a horror film. Gilgamesh and Enkidu are like the audience, projecting their fear onto this currently unknown adversary. Shamash even tells Enkidu and Gilgamesh that once Humbaba has adorned his seven 'terrors' he is unbeatable. Humbaba's very essence is fear.

Once they do come face to face with Humbaba, Gilgamesh again appeals to Shamash for assistance. Gilgamesh's plea for help undercuts his heroic bravado and boasting prior to arriving at the Cedar Forest, suggesting a possible naiveté on his part. However, Gilgamesh also knows that Humbaba is no friend of Shamash, and this insight allows him to appeal to Shamash with more gravitas. He essentially is performing a divine job or favor for Shamash. While Gilgamesh and Enkidu are ultimately held responsible for Humbaba's death, it benefits Shamash as well.

Finally, with Humbaba subdued with Shamash's help, Gilgamesh is prepared to dispatch the monster. Humbaba pleads for his life, promising to become Gilgamesh's servant. Enkidu sees this and tells Gilgamesh not to listen, to kill Humbaba. Humbaba accuses Enkidu of jealousy, perhaps seeking to divide the two heroes by attacking their relationship. Gilgamesh then kills Humbaba, although it is not clear in some translations how he does this. Some versions have him beheading Humbaba, while some focus on other methods. In other versions of the story, Enkidu kills Humbaba himself.

Companionship and cooperation are important themes in this tablet. Enkidu and Gilgamesh steel themselves for the task by reminding each other that together, they can accomplish anything. This concept, that no one who has a friend is truly alone, is mirrored cruelly in later tablets when Gilgamesh finds himself alone without Enkidu. With him at his side, fear and doubt can be pushed to the farthest reaches of his mind.

This confidence becomes arrogance at times, too. Gilgamesh and Enkidu decide to enter a sacred forest, forbidden to mortals, to begin cutting down trees. They wish to build monuments out of these trees, monuments to memorialize themselves and their adventures. This hubris does not go unpunished, as Enkidu soon will learn. Humbaba, facing death, curses Enkidu and warns both heroes that their transgressions will not go unnoticed by the gods.

# Summary and Analysis of Tablet VI and Tablet VII

## Summary

Upon his return to Uruk Gilgamesh bathes his body and dons a clean robe and cloak, and anoints himself with oil. His appearance is so attractive that Ishtar, the goddess of love and war, is overcome with lust. She pleads with Gilgamesh to be her husband. She promises him vast riches if he impregnates her. She tells him they will live together in a house made of cedar, and that she will give him a lapis lazuli chariot with golden wheels.

Gilgamesh pointedly refuses her advances. He says he has nothing to offer her, since, as a goddess, she has everything she could ever want. He tells her he knows of the fate of her other human lovers, and is aware of how fickle her love can be. Gilgamesh recounts the story of Tammuz, the shepherd, who was a captive in the underworld and is mourned in festivals every year. Another shepherd she loved became a bird with broken wings, unable to fly. A goat-herder who loved her was turned into a wolf. When her father's gardener, Ishullanu, rejected her advances, she turned him into a frog. Gilgamesh asks why he should expect to be treated any better.

Ishtar is furious. She goes to her father, Anu, and mother, Antum, and demands that they let her use the Bull of Heaven to punish Gilgamesh. Her father refuses, stating that what Gilgamesh said was true. Ishtar is only further enraged. She threatens to free the dead from the underworld so they can feast on the living. Anu warns her that the bull will also bring a famine. Ishtar assures him that she has made provisions for the people and the flocks of Uruk, and he gives in.

Ishtar unleashes the Bull of Heaven. The city of Uruk trembles as, bellowing and snorting, it comes down from the sky. A crack opens up in the earth, and one hundred men fall into it and die. Again the bull bellows and again the ground cracks open. One hundred more men are swallowed up. The third time this happens, Enkidu attacks the bull. The bull slobbers all over him and whips him with its tail, coated in excrement. Enkidu grabs it by its horns and wrestles with it. He calls out to Gilgamesh, who joins him, and they fight the bull together. At last, Enkidu seizes its filthy tail and holds the monster still so that Gilgamesh can thrust his sword between its shoulders and kill it. The heroes then cut out its heart and offer it as a sacrifice to Shamash the sun god.

Ishtar appears on the walls of the city and curses the two friends. Enkidu picks up one of the bull's bloody haunches and hurls it at her. He threatens that if she were closer, he would do the same to her. While Ishtar and her followers, the temple prostitutes, mourn the bull, Gilgamesh gathers his craftsmen and shows them how beautifully the gods had made the creature, how thickly its horns were coated with lapis lazuli. Gilgamesh removes the horns and fills them with oil, which he offers in sacrifice to his father, Lugulbanda. Then he hangs them on the wall of his palace as a trophy.

Gilgamesh and Enkidu again bathe and wash the bull's blood from their bodies in the Euphrates. That night, Enkidu has a dream that the gods are meeting in council. He awakens suddenly and asks Gilgamesh why the gods would do this.

Tablet VII introduces more details regarding Enkidu's dream. In it, the gods are angry with him and Gilgamesh and they meet to decide what should be done with them. Anu, Ishtar's father, decrees that someone must be punished for killing Humbaba and the Bull of Heaven. Only one of the companions, however, must die. Enlil, Humbaba's master and the god of earth, wind, and air, feels that Enkidu should be the one to die. Shamash, the sun god, defends the heroes, saying that he had influenced their actions in the Cedar Forest. Enlil is angered and accuses Shamash of taking their side and behaving like a mortal instead of a god. Therefore, it is decided that Enkidu must die.

Soon thereafter, Enkidu becomes ill, proving the dream true. Burdened with regret, Enkidu curses Shamhat for civilizing him. He curses the cedar gate that he and Gilgamesh brought back from the Cedar Forest. He states that he would have cut it to pieces with an axe if he had known this would happen. Gilgamesh promises his friend that he will build him an even greater monument than the cedar gate. He will erect an enormous statue of Enkidu, made entirely of gold.

Enkidu curses the trapper who first spotted him at the watering hole and says he hopes his hunting pits are filled in and his traps are unset. Shamash, hearing Enkidu's cries, finally answers. He asks why Enkidu curses the harlot, since if it had not been for her, Enkidu would have never tasted the rich foods of the palace, never worn beautiful clothes, and never known Gilgamesh's friendship. Shamash tells Enkidu that when he dies, Gilgamesh will wander the earth, undone by grief. Enkidu is comforted by Shamash's words and retracts his curse, offering a blessing instead for Shamhat.

The next morning, lying on his deathbed, Enkidu tells Gilgamesh of another terrible dream. In the dream, he was all alone on a dark plain, and a man with a lion's head and an eagle's talons seized him. He fought this creature, but it overpowered him and changed him into a birdlike creature. Then he was dragged down to the underworld. There he saw kings, gods, and priests, all of them dressed in feathers. All of them were living in total darkness. They ate dirt instead of food. Queen Ereshkigal, the ruler of the underworld, sat on her throne, and Belit-Seri, the scribe of the gods, whose tablet tells everyone's fate, knelt before her. Enkidu says the queen looked at them and asked who led them there. Enkidu tells Gilgamesh that he would have been blessed if he had died in battle, because those who die in battle die a glorious death. Enkidu's condition slowly worsens and he suffers for twelve days before he dies.

**Analysis**

Tablet VI reveals a great deal about the importance of Ishtar, the goddess of love, and her mortal lovers. In response to Ishtar's advances, Gilgamesh explains he knows all about her past human lovers who became animals—a shepherd who was changed into a broken-winged bird, a goat herder who became a wolf, a gardener who became a frog. In particular, Gilgamesh mentions Tammuz, a mortal shepherd who becomes a god after his relationship with Ishtar. After his death, he goes to the underworld. Reasons for his death vary from translation to translation, but Ishtar is generally at fault in most traditions.

Gilgamesh's rejection of Ishtar is infuriating to her but also embarrassing. He states aloud the truth about her reputation. Ishtar appears to be more insulted by the revelation of this information than she is by Gilgamesh's initial rejection. When Anu, her father, comments that everything Gilgamesh asserted is true, Ishtar's reaction betrays her feelings. She is, after all, the goddess of love. To have her divine reputation questioned in this manner is extremely insulting but also threatening.

Gilgamesh's list of Ishtar's ex-lovers suggests that Ishtar knows little of love, and perhaps that she should not be worshipped as she currently is. This is no small matter considering that Uruk holds a temple for Ishtar at its very center. Gilgamesh is taking a grave risk by speaking this way to Ishtar. He is challenging the authority of the gods and questioning their very place in a power structure he has heretofore helped to maintain.

The Bull of Heaven is sometimes also called Gugalanna. Gugulanna was the first husband of Ereshkigal, the Goddess of the Netherworld. Ishtar's emotionally charged decision to use the Bull of Heaven to punish Gilgamesh is met with skepticism by Anu, her father. He agrees with Gilgamesh's assessment of Ishtar's reputation, further enraging her. She counters with a serious threat: to release the dead into the land of the living. Anu relents but is concerned about the destruction the Bull will bring. Ishtar tells him she has made provisions to see the people through a period of drought. The distinction that the responsible party should be punished, rather than innocent bystanders, for his insults is revisited in Utnapishtim's story of the flood in a later tablet. Although Anu and Ishtar are engaged in a heated conversation, both are aware of their responsibilities as gods and the power that they can wield.

After Gilgamesh and Enkidu defeat the Bull of Heaven, Ishtar curses them from the walls of the city. Enkidu tears of a haunch of the Bull and throws it at her, telling her he would do the same to her if he could. This compounds their insult against Ishtar and more directly implicates Enkidu's involvement. Gilgamesh takes the Bull's horns to the craftsmen of Uruk. They marvel at how they were made and at how beautiful they are. He hangs them as a trophy for his chambers. His pride over his accomplishments can be interpreted as a certain lack of respect towards the divine. The Bull of Heaven is a divine instrument, but Gilgamesh slays it and dismantles the body. Both heroes seem to have forgotten their place.

Enkidu and Gilgamesh return to bathe in the Euphrates after their victory. The people of Uruk celebrate their conquests and Gilgamesh boasts that he and Enkidu are best. This final bit of hubris is soon met with a foreboding dream that Enkidu has. In it the gods are meeting together in council. Enkidu awakens and asks Gilgamesh why they would be doing this. Enkidu seems to have suddenly realized the possibility of severe repercussions for their actions. It is notable that Gilgamesh, who has had many dreams of events to come, does not dream of this event. His ignorance on this matter foreshadows how shaken he will be by Enkidu's death. It is also the first dream that either hero has that is not metaphorical in nature. As Tablet VII will show, the gods do actually convene to discuss the actions of the two heroes.

The decision by the gods to punish Enkidu introduces another theme in the epic: the gods can and will act without explanation or reason. Some translations state that Gilgamesh's semi-divine nature is a factor in their decision to spare him and select Enkidu for death. This theme is visited again when Utnapishtim tells Gilgamesh of the Flood brought upon humanity without explanation. The irony of this behavior is that the gods punish the heroes for their behavior while rarely justifying their own. Ishtar becomes jealous and vengeful and releases the Bull of Heaven. Her target is Gilgamesh but hundreds die before Enkidu is able to subdue the Bull, yet there are no repercussions for Ishtar's decisions and she does not exhibit remorse for the men that died. The gods answer only to one another, not to another higher being, so their power is largely unchecked.

Enkidu curses his predicament by blaming Shamhat and the trapper. Because of them, he contends, he was removed from the wilderness where he was content and put on a path leading to his eventual downfall. The knowledge he has gained through his civilization has augmented his suffering rather than helped subdue it. It is possible that the authors were using this as an analogy about what was then modern urban life. The life of animals may have appeared to be far less complex and more easily enjoyed. It also again reflects the Biblical metaphor of Eden. Had humanity been able to stay in Eden, none of us would have to know suffering.

Shamash hears Enkidu's cries and comforts him by reminding Enkidu that if not for Shamhat and the trapper, Enkidu would not have tasted the best that civilization has to offer. He would also never have met his friend Gilgamesh. He tells Enkidu, essentially, that he is beloved by Gilgamesh and that when he passes away Gilgamesh will be full of sorrow. Although Enkidu's demise is still imminent, he is comforted by Shamash's words. He realizes that he has enjoyed some of the most important things in life, namely love and friendship. He recants his curse and offers a blessing instead for Shamhat. This suggests that curses and blessings carried great weight in the ancient Mesopotamian world. Such words were not invoked lightly, and, if uttered, were believed to have consequences. Finally, having attained some sense of peace, Enkidu passes away, leaving Gilgamesh alone. The lesson now imparted to Gilgamesh is that despite his great strength and reputation, death is inescapable.

# Summary and Analysis of Tablet VIII and Tablet IX

## Summary

Gilgamesh is crushed by Enkidu's death. He rips his clothes and tears his hair. He circles Enkidu's body restlessly and proclaims his sadness. He touches his friend's heart and feels nothing. Gilgamesh calls on the animals, Shamhat, and the elders of the city to all mourn the loss of Enkidu. The rivers, the forests, and the farmers all mourn Enkidu's death.

Gilgamesh then summons the artisans of Uruk together. He instructs them to build a statue of gold to commemorate Enkidu. He eulogizes Enkidu with kind words and remains by Enkidu's body until he sees a worm crawls out of its nose. He tears off his royal garb garments with anger and dons filthy animal skins. He pours honey into a carnelian bowl, places some butter in a bowl of lapis lazuli, and makes an offering to Shamash.

Soon thereafter Gilgamesh journeys into the wilderness, just as Shamash had told Enkidu he would. He wanders alone aimlessly in anguish until he formulates a new plan. Gilgamesh decides to seek out Utnapishtim, a legendary figure who survived the flood that almost ended life on Earth. Utnapishtim was granted immortality by the gods. Gilgamesh wishes to learn this secret too. Utnapishtim lives a far-off place forbidden to mortal beings. Gilgamesh's journey there will be dangerous.

On his way to find Utnapishtim, Gilgamesh enters a mountain pass at night. The moon lights the path, and Gilgamesh sees lions circling about. Afraid, he appeals to Sin, the Moon god, for protection. He descends on the lions and kills them with a violent passion. In some versions, he dreams of a vague battle with an enemy who stands over him. It is unclear who this figure is or who wins the battle.

Gilgamesh arrives at Mount Mashu, the twin-peaked mountain. One peak faces west, toward the setting of the sun, and the other faces east toward its rising point. Two monsters, a Scorpion-man and his wife, guard the gates to a passage that runs under Mashu. The male monster tells his wife that any person who dares to come here must be a god. His wife senses that Gilgamesh is two-thirds a god and one-third mortal. The male monster asks Gilgamesh to identify himself and explain why he has traveled to Mashu.

Gilgamesh tells the monsters his story and his desire to see Utnapishtim. The Scorpion-man informs him that Utnapishtim lives on the other side of the mountain. To get there, Gilgamesh must use a passage that runs through the mountain. Shamash uses this same passage each night to travel back to the point where the sun rises every morning. Gilgamesh must travel the entire length of the passage in complete darkness. It will take him an entire day to do (Twelve "double-hours"). The

Scorpion-man warns Gilgamesh that the way is treacherous and that no mortal has ever attempted it. Gilgamesh will be the first. He tells Gilgamesh that he must endure the tests of this long passage and lets him pass.

Gilgamesh walks through the mountain in absolute darkness. He cannot see in front of him or behind him. He walks the first, second, and third double hour in total blackness and struggles to breathe in the hot darkness. He walks four, five, and six double hours with the north wind blowing in his face. As the eleventh double hour approaches, the darkness begins to fade. At the end of the twelfth double hour, Gilgamesh emerges from the tunnel into the sunlight, breathing fresh air. He sees a beautiful garden filled with flowers of all colors. Beyond the garden, he sees the sea.

## Analysis

As Gilgamesh mourns for Enkidu, he undergoes a physical transformation that makes his appearance similar to that of Enkidu's. Gilgamesh tears his hair and clothes and eventually puts on filthy animal skins. Whereas Enkidu's civilization made his appearance more like Gilgamesh's, here the process is exactly the opposite. Gilgamesh reverts to a more savage state. His appearance suggests that he is trying to keep Enkidu alive in his own mind by becoming him.

Gilgamesh's language while memorializing his friend also directly correlates to Enkidu's wilderness roots. He deliberately invokes visions of the meadows and plains and the animals that inhabit them. These verses simultaneously speak to Enkidu's innocence and his humanity. Enkidu was new to the ways of man when he met his demise but he was beloved by all that knew him in that short time. While he may have died a man, he is mourned by both the civilized and natural worlds.

Gilgamesh struggles to accept Enkidu's death but is also in denial of death itself. When Gilgamesh sees a worm emerge from Enkidu's nose, he can no longer deny what is happening: his friend is dead. He sees that one day he too will die. This drives him to seek a way out, to cheat death itself. Therefore, Gilgamesh decides to find Utnapishtim and makes his way to Mashu. On his way, he encounters lions, and asks Sin, the god of the moon, to protect him. In some translations, this occurs in a dream while in others it is an actual event. In some versions of the dream, Gilgamesh is frightened but it is unclear whom he faces.

Upon reaching Mashu and entering the mountain passage, he endures a suffocating darkness. This is a common archetypal feature in many hero myths or stories. Gilgamesh's initial quest against Humbaba and the Bull of Heaven has proven his heroic abilities, but now he is truly tested in a terrifying experience. The hero generally must face this challenge alone, and Gilgamesh is no exception. He is surrounded by darkness, and he cannot see behind him or in front of him. His solitude is inescapable. There is literally nowhere else to go, or anyone else to turn to for aid. The darkness becomes a literal symbolization of his solitude.

Having endured this, Gilgamesh reaches the other side of the mountain passage and finds a beautiful garden filled with fruit and flowers of bright colors. Beyond it, he can see the sea. Gilgamesh has entered a new world. His passage through the dark passage mimics the birth process itself and his emergence on the other side is a symbolic rebirth. While Gilgamesh still mourns for Enkidu's loss, he is ultimately seeking out his own salvation. He may believe that immortality is the answer to his problems but he will find that salvation takes on another form.

# Summary and Analysis of Tablet X

## Summary

Siduri, a barmaid, keeps a tavern overlooking the sea. In the distance, she sees Gilgamesh coming toward her. His appearance frightens her. He is wearing animal skins, and his face is weathered. Siduri barricades herself inside the tavern. Gilgamesh pounds on the door and threatens to kick it down. He tells Siduri who he is and Siduri asks him why he looks the way he does if he is indeed the great Gilgamesh. Gilgamesh tells her that he is grieving for the loss of his friend, Enkidu, with whom he slayed the demon Humbaba and the Bull of Heaven. He says that Enkidu has been overtaken by the fate that awaits all humankind—he is turned to clay. Gilgamesh asks Siduri if that is what must happen to him as well.

Siduri opens the tavern door and invites him in, telling him that only the gods live forever. She invites him to clean up and to eat and drink. Gilgamesh instead says he wants to find Utnapishtim and asks Siduri where he can find him. Siduri tells Gilgamesh that Shamash the sun god crosses the sea every day, but no mortal has ever been able to follow him. Siduri says that even if he miraculously survived the crossing, he would then face the poisonous Waters of Death, which only Urshanabi, Utnapishtim's boatman, can cross.

Urshanabi lives on an island somewhere on these waters where he guards the Urnu-snakes and the Stone Things. She urges him to abandon this quest, telling him that immortality was never meant for anyone but the gods. However, Gilgamesh cannot be convinced otherwise. Finally, Siduri gives him directions to the island where Urshanabi lives and tells him that perhaps he will take Gilgamesh across the waters to see Utnapishtim upon seeing Gilgamesh's face. If he refuses, she says, Gilgamesh must abandon this quest.

Gilgamesh sets off to find Urshanabi. When he arrives near the place where the Urnu-snakes and the Stone Things reside, he attacks them with his axe and dagger, destroying them. He then battles a winged creature but manages to defeat it as well. The sounds of battle garner Urshanabi's attention and he follows them to their source.

Gilgamesh introduces himself to Urshanabi. Urshanabi studies Gilgamesh's face and questions him about his appearance. Gilgamesh tells him about Enkidu, his grief, his fear of death, and his desire to find Utnapishtim.

Urshanabi says he will take Gilgamesh to Utnapishtim, but that Gilgamesh has made the task much more difficult because he has destroyed the Stone Things and the Urnu-snakes, which propelled and protected his boat. Instead, Urshanabi says, Gilgamesh must go into the forest and fashion hundreds of poles. Each pole must be exactly sixty cubits in length (approximately ninety feet). Urshanabi instructs him to fit the poles with rings and cover them with pitch, and then they will attempt the voyage.

Gilgamesh cuts the poles, and they sail off together across the perilous sea. In three days, they sail as far as an ordinary boat would have sailed in two months. When they arrive at the Waters of Death, the boatman tells Gilgamesh to use the punting poles but to be sure that his hands do not touch the water. Gilgamesh steers the boat through the Waters of Death. His great strength causes him to break all of the poles. In some translations, the poles disintegrate in the Waters of Death. When the last pole is ruined, he takes off the animal skin he wears and holds it up as a sail.

In the distance, they can see a shore. An old man stands on the shore, watching the boat approach. The old man wonders who the stranger is with Urshanabi. When they get out of the boat, the old man asks Gilgamesh to identify himself. Gilgamesh tells the old man his story as well. The old man asks Gilgamesh why he grieves over mortality—nothing lives forever. He explains that the gods established that humanity would suffer death, and that when the gods give life, they decide the day of death. He says that death is our inescapable destiny, even if we do not know when it will happen.

**Analysis**

Siduri the veiled barmaid is a traditional figure in Mesopotamian mythology and poetry, and in the Hurrian language, her name means "young woman." The goddess of winemaking and beer brewing, she is usually considered a manifestation of Ishtar. Her warmth and kindness to Gilgamesh throughout this episode are remarkable considering how Gilgamesh treated Ishtar prior to Enkidu's death.

Scholars have not been able to determine what the Stone Things and the Urnu-snakes mentioned in this tablet are exactly or why Gilgamesh destroys them. Some translations suggest the Stone Things were actual stones that were used to construct a bridge. Others suggest they were magnetite. The tablets are incomplete on this topic. The Winged creature that Gilgamesh encounters is Utnapishtim in some versions of the story.

Both Siduri and Urshanabi have no idea who Gilgamesh is when they see him, suggesting his appearance is truly repulsive. Even after explaining his story to them, they both independently tell him that his quest is pointless and that he should turn back. When Gilgamesh finally reaches the old man, he tells Gilgamesh that death is inescapable.

As we will learn in the next tablet, the old man is in fact Utnapishtim. Even though Utnapishtim has been granted immortality himself, he advises Gilgamesh against seeking it out. This suggests that Utnapishtim's experience with immortality has not been completely positive. Immortality itself robs life of urgency and meaning. Utnapishtim will live forever, but this limits his personal ambition greatly. He has no endpoint in his life to fear, but he also has no motivations. There is no deadline.

In a way, death gives meaning to life. Without it, we have little reason to consider how our lives are lived and how we will be remembered. Utnapishtim may also realize that immortality will not allow Gilgamesh to become the king he is meant to be. Utnapishtim has escaped death, but he will not help Gilgamesh to do the same. Utnapishtim says that Gilgamesh inherited his father's mortality and, like everything else in the mortal world, he is subject to death. Gilgamesh must continue to live as a mortal and accept death as a part of life.

# Summary and Analysis of Tablet XI

**Summary**

Gilgamesh soon realizes that the old man he has been speaking to is in fact Utnapishtim. He is surprised that Utnapishtim appears as just another man, whereas Gilgamesh had expected to face a terrible demon. Gilgamesh asks Utnapishtim to explain how it came to be that he was allowed to live as an immortal, and how Gilgamesh can do the same.

Utnapishtim explains that long ago he was once the king of city called Shuruppak, a city that was situated on the Euphrates. The gods Anu, Enlil, Ninerta, Ea, and Ennugi met in council and decided to bring a flood to destroy the city. Ea whispers to Utnapishtim through his house walls to abandon his belongings and instead build a boat. Ea gave him dimensions for this boat. It would have six decks and be of an enormous size, about 180 feet high. On this boat, Ea said, Utnapishtim should bring his family and the seed of every species.

Utnapishtim asked Ea what he should tell the people of Shuruppak, since he needs help to construct the boat, and people would naturally have questions as to his intent. Ea told Utnapishtim to tell the people that he must leave the city because Enlil is angry with him and that he must find a new home and a new divine protector. Ea says to tell the people that he will be Utnapishtim's patron and that Utnapishtim will travel to Apsu, the abyss. Ea also instructed Utnapishtim to tell the people of Shuruppak that a flood of bounty and good fortune would greet the city upon Utnapishtim's departure. Food and drink would be plentiful with more than enough bread and fish for everyone.

The people of Shuruppak, young and old, came out to help with the construction of the boat. Each day Utnapishtim would sacrifice a bull or lamb and beer and wine were in great supply for a great feast. Each day ended with a festival-like celebration. In just seven days, the boat was complete. Utnapishtim loaded all his belongings on to the vessel and after some difficulty was able to cast off.

Storm clouds gathered as Utnapishtim set the boat adrift. Utnapishtim shields himself inside the boat with the help of Puzuramurri, the caulker. He gives the caulker his home as thanks and settles in while the storm rages outside. Utnapishtim describes a terrible storm that lasts for seven days. The storm is so thick that the gods cannot even see the earth from the heavens. Ishtar cries out in anguish over the loss of humanity.

When the storm finally subsides, Utnapishtim looked out but saw nothing moving. There were no signs of life anywhere but he sees something in the distance that may be an island. He tries to steer the boat in that direction but finds that the boat is caught on the peak of Mount Nisir. After being stuck there for seven days

Utnapishtim releases a dove into the air to see if it can find a place to land. It returns to the boat. Utnapishtim next frees a swallow into the air but it too returns to the boat. Finally, Utnapishtim releases a raven and the bird does not return this time. After that, Utnapishtim released all the birds.

Upon reaching shore, Utnapishtim prepares a sacrifice and offers libations to the gods. The gods descend and gather around the altar. Ishtar tells Utnapishtim that she will never forget the flood and its terrible price. She says that Enlil is forbidden from attending this ceremony. Enlil does appear, however, and upon seeing the boat and Utnapishtim becomes enraged, demanding to know how one man was able to survive. Ninurta tells Enlil that Ea has the answer.

Ea reprimands Enlil for inflicting a punishment on all of humanity for what one man may have done to upset him. Ea states that the punishment does not fit the crime. Ea says that he did not tell Utnapishtim of the gods' plan, but that Utnapishtim guessed it and acted wisely. Ea suggest a reward is in order for Utnapishtim. Enlil then took Utnapishtim and his wife aboard the boat and made them kneel before him. He touches their foreheads and decrees that their mortality has ended and that they are admitted into the company of the gods, to live forever. He tells them they will now journey to the Faraway, a place beyond the world of mortals, where all the rivers originate, and reside there.

Utnapishtim then asks Gilgamesh what *he* has done that would require the gods to convene and grant him immortality. He challenges Gilgamesh to stay awake for six days and seven nights. Gilgamesh accepts and seats himself, ready to take the test. As soon as he does, an ocean mist comes over him from the shore and he falls asleep. Utnapishtim remarks to his wife that the hero who seeks eternal life now sleeps. She asks him to wake Gilgamesh and tell him to return to his home. Instead, Utnapishtim tells her to bake a loaf of bread each day and lay it next to Gilgamesh for each day that he sleeps, as proof that he has been asleep. She also marks the wall to record each day. Gilgamesh sleeps for seven days and when he awakes finds seven loaves of bread by his head but denies having slept at all. Utnapishtim directs his attention to the loaves of bread. The first is crusty and stale, while the most recent is fresh. Gilgamesh is demoralized again and asks Utnapishtim what he should do.

Utnapishtim tells Urshanabi the boatman that he is now forbidden from this shore. He must never return. Instead, he says, he tells Urshanabi to take Gilgamesh to bathe and dress himself appropriately before accompanying him back to the city of Uruk. As Gilgamesh and Urshanabi begin their journey back, Utnapishtim's wife implores her husband to give Gilgamesh something to take back with him, considering the long journey he has made to get there. Utnapishtim agrees and tells Gilgamesh of a magic plant called How-the-Old-Man-Once-Again-Becomes-A-Young-Man that will restore Gilgamesh to his youth. Utnapishtim says this plant can be found at the bottom of the sea.

Gilgamesh ties heavy stones to his feet and descends into the waters. He locates the plant and pulls it out. He cuts the stones from his feet and surfaces with the plant. He tells Urshanabi that he will take the plant to the elders of Uruk and use its rejuvenating powers on them. Then he will partake and once again be strongest and youngest.

The two men begin their journey to Uruk. On their way, they come across a spring and Gilgamesh decides to bathe in its waters. He leaves the magic plant on shore where a serpent comes by and takes the plant, shedding its skin as it does so. When Gilgamesh returns from bathing, he is heartbroken to find that the plant is missing. He cries to Urshanabi that his efforts have been in vain.

Finally, the two men continue and reach Uruk. As they enter the city, Gilgamesh shows Urshanabi the walls of the city and the temple of Ishtar. He shows him the fields and orchards. He speaks with pride of Uruk, the city of Gilgamesh.

**Analysis**

There is an obvious parallel between Utnapishtim's story and the account of the flood in the Bible. It should be noted that some scholars also believe that an editor added the flood story, based on the Epic of Atrahasis, to Tablet XI. In both Utnapishtim's story and the Bible account, a large boat is constructed and filled with all the living beings on earth. In both stories, the boat comes to rest or is caught on a mountain peak. However, God chose Noah because of Noah's exemplary righteousness. The rest of humanity is punished in the Bible for behaving wickedly. In Utnapishtim's story, the gods give no reason for the flood. The decision appears to be arbitrary. In some older versions of the story, Enlil complains that humanity is too noisy and prevents him from sleeping. This appears to be a character trait of Enlil as he also decides that Enkidu must be the one to die, also without a concrete reason. Utnapishtim also does not ask the gods why the flood is coming.

Following the flood, all the gods display regret over their actions except for Enlil, who is angry that anyone has survived. He is quickly reprimanded by Ea. Ea's cleverness is on show in this tablet, as it is he who gives Utnapishtim knowledge of the flood to come and instructs him to build a boat, complete with the dimensions necessary. Ea even provides Utnapishtim with an excuse in case anyone asks why the boat is being built. Linguistic scholars have noted that when Utnapishtim tells the people of Shuruppak that they will enjoy a great harvest of wheat and bread, he uses a pun that almost serves as a clue. The word for "bread" in Akkadian is very similar to the word for "darkness" and the word or "wheat" very similar to the word for "misfortune."

Utnapishtim's story illustrates that humanity perseveres. Even if each of us is to meet our own end eventually, the human cycle of life continues indefinitely. Although Enlil is initially upset that Utnapishtim has survived, the other gods are thankful that humanity has not been destroyed. For this, Enlil rewards Utnapishtim and his wife with the gift of immortality. This suggests a relationship between humankind and the gods that was mutually beneficial. Without the devotion of their human subjects, the gods of ancient Mesopotamia seemed to be without power. Some translations of the story state that the gods descend on Utnapishtim's sacrifice offering not having eaten for days because no offerings had been made to them. The people, in turn, rely on the gods for assistance and protection. Both need the other to survive and prosper.

Gilgamesh now has to understand that death is a necessity, another part of life. Utnapishtim challenges Gilgamesh to stay awake for six days and seven nights (some translations state that he simply says for seven days). This challenge illustrates Utnapishtim's point poetically. Sleep is similar to death: a prostate body could be a sleeping person or one who is dead. It is metaphorically close to death, but also a necessary part of life. Utnapishtim's analogy is that one cannot live without sleep, just as one cannot live without death. However, Utnapishtim knows he will need proof to demonstrate that Gilgamesh has failed the test. When Gilgamesh sees the loaves of bread left out for him, he is distraught.

After obtaining the magic plant, Gilgamesh tells Urshanabi that he wants to take it to the elders of Uruk to restore their youth. This signals a change in Gilgamesh. It is the first time he mentions doing something for the benefit of others. While his motives are still selfish, to restore his own youth, he does not mean to keep the plant to himself. He may be able to save others from death and reduce the suffering of others around him.

The serpent that steals the plant as Gilgamesh bathes again conjures up a Biblical allegory, but there is a difference. The serpent in the Bible uses forbidden fruit to tempt Eve, eventually leading to Adam and Eve's ejection from Eden. The serpent in Gilgamesh's story steals the plant from Gilgamesh, who now has no choice but to face his fate. Rather than presenting a challenge to Gilgamesh, the serpent's actions allow Gilgamesh to free himself of his attachment to immortality. His transformation is almost complete. The serpent sheds its skin as it takes the plant, attaining its own youth. This shedding may also reflect Gilgamesh's need to shed his old ways and become a better king.

Upon returning to Uruk Gilgamesh looks upon the city with new eyes. He sees the city walls and its temples and realizes that it is his home, a testament to humanity, but also to him if he can rule it well. Most translations of the epic mention the temple of Ishtar specifically, suggesting that Gilgamesh has made peace with the goddess after his previous transgressions. It also suggests that the story is emphasizing the importance of women in human society. Two women, Siduri and Utnapishtim's wife, take pity on Gilgamesh when he is at his lowest and offer their kindness as he tries to come to terms with his predicament. Women give birth to and nurture the young, allowing the all-important cycle of life to renew.

# Summary and Analysis of Tablet XII

**Summary**

A twelfth tablet exists that is not part of the main body of the epic and is not included in some translations and versions. Sin-Leqi-Unnini added the tablet to the poem, but it is unclear why. It does not correspond to the rest of the poem and contradicts some of the events outlined in it.

Gilgamesh drops a drumstick through a hole in the floor of a carpenter's home and it falls into the Nether World. Enkidu, who is still alive in this tablet, offers to venture down and retrieve it. Gilgamesh warns Enkidu that if he goes to the Nether World he must not do anything to attract the attention of anyone, or the dead will overtake him. Enkidu enters the Nether World but does not heed any of Gilgamesh's advice, doing exactly the opposite. Ereshkigal, the Queen of the Nether World, seizes him with the Cry of the Dead. Some translations suggest that Ereshkigal exposes her breasts and forces Enkidu to make love to her.

Gilgamesh grieves the loss of Enkidu and approaches Enlil for aid. Enlil refuses and Gilgamesh makes his way to Sin, the moon god for help. Sin ignores his cries for help. Finally, Gilgamesh goes to Ea for help. Ea intercedes and allows Enkidu's spirit to rise up and escape the Nether World. Gilgamesh inquires about the Nether World. Enkidu tells him that it is terrible and that if he tells Gilgamesh, Gilgamesh will sit down and weep. Gilgamesh implores Enkidu to tell him anyway. Enkidu says that vermin eat at his body. Gilgamesh sits down and weeps.

After a while, Gilgamesh inquires about the fate of different people: the man with no children, the man with one son, the man with six sons, the man who died in battle, and a man who left no one behind to remember him. Enkidu tells him the fate of each, explaining that the man with no sons is miserable, the man with six sons is happy, and that the man who left no one behind eats garbage. No dog would eat what he eats.

**Analysis**

As in the main story, Enkidu finds himself in the Nether World by upsetting mystical forces. Instead of angering Ishtar, he pays no attention to Gilgamesh's warning, and he is taken by the Cry of the Dead. The carpenter's home and drumstick in the beginning of this tablet do not have a clear interpretation. It is not explained why the heroes are there or what significance the drum takes. The fact that the use of these objects opens a hole into the Nether World suggests that the drum could have been used in a ceremony to speak to the dead as one would in a séance or shamanistic tradition.

Once Enkidu is taken by the Cry of the Dead, it is again Ea that helps him and

Gilgamesh. This allows Gilgamesh to learn about the fate of those in the Nether World and imparts the same core lesson to him as the main body of the epic. Enkidu's tale about those he has seen in the Nether World emphasizes the importance of relationships in the living world. Those who leave a family behind fare far better than those who have no one to remember them. They feed on garbage and are regarded as lower than dogs. Enkidu's example does not speak of individuals who have attained happiness through great wealth.

# Suggested Essay Questions

1. **Enkidu is civilized through his encounter with Shamhat, a prostitute. As opposed to our own society, what does this say about views toward sexuality and femininity in ancient Mesopotamia?**

Rather than being seen as a negative attribute, Shamhat's sexuality and its ties to the temple cement her importance in Mesopotamian society. She is a means to tame Enkidu as opposed to a means for him to behave like an animal. Throughout the poem, the role of women is unavoidable and important. Although Enkidu and Gilgamesh insult Ishtar, Gilgamesh specifically points out her temple to Urshanabi.

2. **Compare and contrast the role of the serpent and the flood in the Bible and the Epic of Gilgamesh. What similarities and differences can be found?**

In both books the serpent is presented negatively; a force that deprives humanity of some pleasure or immortality. In the Bible, the serpent is a deliberate force of temptation, and Adam and Eve are cast out as sinners. It is clearly depicted as an evil presence. In Gilgamesh, Gilgamesh's own carelessness deprives him of immortality. In his case, the role of the serpent is necessary for him to move past his feelings toward life and death and become a better king, making this serpent less of a villain and more a catalyst for change.

The flood stories in both texts are very similar, and some scholars believe that they refer to a singular event. However, there are differences between the accounts.

3. **What does Gilgamesh's and Enkidu's constant struggle and defiance of the gods tell us about how the gods were viewed in Gilgamesh's time? Are the consequences that both characters face worth the risk each takes?**

The gods as depicted in Gilgamesh's story, as well as Utnapishtim's, are presented as being easily angered and vengeful. Part of Gilgamesh's heroic pedigree is inherent in being two-thirds a god himself, but his acts of defiance also speak to a possibly resentful view of the gods among ancient Mesopotamians. The gods are depicted as being difficult to please, sometimes punishing without explanation or meting out punishments that seem far out of proportion to the original offense, as in Utnapishtim's story. Both characters take on large risks by insulting Ishtar, but Gilgamesh is able to face his own mortality and Enkidu is able to learn of the world of humans and of the value of life. Both also come to understand the importance of friendship in life.

4. **What does Humbaba/Huwawa represent? Use examples from the story**

**to support your position.**

Humbaba represents fear and the unknown. Both Enkidu and Gilgamesh experience great fear in the cedar forest when they are about to face Humbaba. They support one another with encouraging words when the other is frightened. One can also argue that Humbaba represents nature itself. As guardian of the Cedar Forest, he has a duty to protect it from harm. Gilgamesh and Enkidu together represent civilization. They seek to tame the natural world for their own purposes.

5. **At various points in the story, dreams foretell events to come. What do these passages reveal about how dreams were valued in Mesopotamian culture? What do they tell us about the dreamer's state of mind?**

It is obvious from the text that dreams were regarded as important markers that should be interpreted. It seems fair to say that the ancient Mesopotamians lent a good deal of credibility to them in their day-to-day lives. As Gilgamesh dreams of the meteor and the axe in anticipation of his meeting with Enkidu, he turns to his mother for an interpretation of his dreams. While she informs him of the imminent arrival of Enkidu, it could also be that Gilgamesh is lonely and looking for a companion. Enkidu dreams of the gods deciding his death and of what the underworld will be like. His state of mind is one of absolute fear of his defiance of the gods.

6. **Although Gilgamesh faces his own mortality upon Enkidu's death, he also must now face a life without his friend. Why is this also of importance? What does it teach Gilgamesh about life and the spirit of endurance?**

Beyond teaching Gilgamesh that his own life must end, Enkidu's death also forces Gilgamesh to continue living the life he still has left. He is initially so distraught over Enkidu's death that he more or less abandons his kingly duties. Utnapishtim teaches him that life must end, but Gilgamesh also must return to Uruk with the full understanding that his own life must continue if it is to have meaning.

7. **What is the significance of the darkness that Gilgamesh encounters in the passage beneath Mount Mashu on his way to seek Utnapishtim?**

The text repeatedly mentions how Gilgamesh is alone at this point in the story. With nothing else visible around him, Gilgamesh is truly on his own on this quest. He is also completely lost, without obvious direction, fumbling in the dark. This metaphor reiterates Gilgamesh's struggle with the loss of Enkidu. He is suddenly finding himself unsure of how to proceed in life.

8. **Repetition is a frequent technique the author(s) used in the Epic of Gilgamesh, as is the theme of duality. Enkidu and Gilgamesh are near mirrors of each other, for example. They undertake two quests: one against Humbaba, the other against the Bull of Heaven. Discuss other**

**examples of duality and repetition in the story. Why does the epic contain these elements?**

Repetition reinforces themes present in the story, or attributes of a character. Sometimes repetition can also draw contrasts between different events or characters. Besides reinforcing elements in the story, repetition also suggests that these stories may have had a strong oral tradition and were largely passed down in this manner before being committed to these tablets.

Duality also draws comparisons between characters and again reinforces one of the themes of the story: companionship. Enkidu and Gilgamesh are near mirrors of each other. Gilgamesh and Utnapishtim also share some characteristics, not in appearance, but in the knowledge that they both have gained. Enkidu and Gilgamesh embark on two quests. Gilgamesh's journey to the underworld mirrors his quest with Enkidu.

9. **The story begins and ends with a description of the city of Uruk and its walls and other features? What does this signify?**

For Gilgamesh it signals reconciliation with the finite nature of life. He is able to return to where he began and see it, almost with new eyes, and a new appreciation. He accepts his place. It also brings the story full-circle, perhaps an aesthetic choice to mirror the cyclical nature of life.

10. **Comment on Gilgamesh and Enkidu's relationship. Is their love of a sexual nature or a more platonic one? The text describes them as being very close. Why do you think that is?**

Although there is language in the text suggestive of a relationship beyond friendship between the two, there is no direct evidence of a sexual relationship between Gilgamesh and Enkidu. At the same time, Gilgamesh declares a love for Enkidu greater than that for any woman. However, Gilgamesh's sexual appetite for women is established early on in the text, where it is written that he sleeps with newly married brides before their husbands do. It is more likely that as the gods created Enkidu to be a counterweight to Gilgamesh, the characters are able to find in each other an understanding that no one else can provide. Only they are able to comprehend what it is like to be the other.

# The Epic of Atrahasis

The Flood story recounted to Gilgamesh by Utnapishtim is markedly similar to the account of the flood in the Bible. However, an Akkadian epic dating back to the 18th Century BCE features a nearly identical flood story involving a character named Atrahasis. Although the *Epic of Atrahasis* is fragmentary in much the same way the Gilgamesh epic is, there are three tablets which comprise the most complete version of the story.

Atrahasis was a Sumerian King of Shuruppak before the flood. The first tablet of the epic is a creation story, explaining the origin of humankind. The goddess Mami creates humanity out of clay to do the work that lesser gods refuse to do. Tablet II deals with overpopulation, as Enlil uses alternating periods of drought and famine to reduce the population and keep it under control. Enlil eventually decides to destroy humanity with a flood.

Tablet III features an account of the flood, which was likely adapted for the Epic of Gilgamesh. In it, Enki, the god of water, warns Atrahasis of the coming flood. He does this in exactly the same manner that Ea warns Utnapishtim, by speaking to him through the reed walls of his house. He instructs Atrahasis to tear down his home and build a boat. Enki tells Atrahasis that the boat will need multiple decks and must be of great size.

When the boat is complete, Atrahasis boards it with his family and animals. The storm begins and then rages for seven days. When it ends, Atrahasis goes ashore and makes a sacrifice to the gods, again, just as Utnapishtim did. In this version, Enlil is angry with Enki for sharing the secret of the flood with Atrahasis. Enki argues that he has done what was necessary to preserve life. The two gods agree that they must develop another method to control the population, but in this version, they do have a reason for bringing the flood. Utnapishtim's account offers no explanation from the gods for the extermination of humanity.

The similarities are obvious when one compares the contents of Tablet III to that of Tablet XI in Gilgamesh's story. However, Atrahasis's story has no mention of a reward from the gods. This may be because Enki takes the lion's share of the credit for saving humanity, whereas Ea denied telling Utnapishtim anything directly. Regardless, Atrahasis is not granted immortality in the most complete version of the epic.

Many scholars believe this story was directly adapted for use in the *Epic of Gilgamesh*, arguing that the names Atrahasis and Utnapishtim may have even referred to the same individual. Ea addresses Utnapishtim as the "son of Ubartutu," and Atrahasis is also said to be the son of Ubartutu. This strengthens the argument that the flood story in Gilgamesh comes directly from the *Epic of Atrahasis*, but there is still debate among scholars.

# Author of ClassicNote and Sources

Amit Dave, author of ClassicNote. Completed on August 19, 2011, copyright held by GradeSaver.

Updated and revised Bella Wang August 19, 2011. Copyright held by GradeSaver.

David Ferry. Gilgamesh: A New Rendering in English Verse. New York: The Noonday Press, 1992.

Herbert Mason. Gilgamesh. New York: Penguin Putnam, 1970.

Stephen Mitchell. Gilgamesh: A New English Version. New York: Free Press, 2004.

N.K. Sandars. The Epic of Gilgamesh. London: Penguin Books, 1960.

Danny Jackson. "The Epic of Gilgamesh." Bolchazy-Carducci Publishers Inc.. 1997-01-01. 2011-08-11.
<http://books.google.co.uk/books?id=Z_-NXZ814awC&printsec=frontcover#v=onepage&q&

# Essay: Enkidu's Deathbed Realization

**by Anonymous**
**November 01, 2006**

Enkidu's Deathbed Realization

The heartbreaking scenes in the seventh tablet of The Epic of Gilgamesh describe Enkidu's deathbed realization that his friendship with Gilgamesh was a one-sided affair. In this scene, Enkidu lies dying and feeling abandoned by Gilgamesh. In his death throes, "Enkidu's innards were churning / lying there so alone" (Kovacs 64). Just before he dies, Enkidu cries out "my friend hates me...my friend who I saved in battle has now abandoned me" (Kovacs 66). This agonizing deathbed realization of the limitations of their friendship calls for a reevaluation of the nature of the friendship between Gilgamesh and Enkidu.

At the outset, Enkidu and Gilgamesh have such inconsistent roles that Enkidu's deathbed realization seems it should have been obvious. As the story opens, Gilgamesh is described as taking advantage of his subjects. Although the nature of his acts is not entirely clear, we are left with the impression of Gilgamesh as undisciplined and out of control. Guided only by his "stormy heart" and great physical strength, Gilgamesh is not a good ruler and needs to be brought into line. There is no indication in the text that Gilgamesh is seeking a relationship with anyone, let alone a friend. Enkidu was created by Aruru to bring Gilgamesh into line. As ordained by Anu, Enkidu's role is not to satisfy Gilgamesh's need for friendship, but rather to bring Gilgamesh under control.

Enkidu's needs are in sharp contrast to Gilgamesh. Unlike Gilgamesh, Enkidu is looking for a good friend. After his assignation with Shamash, Enkidu realizes that he has lost his animal friends and, "becoming aware of himself, he sought a friend" (Kovacs 10). Although it initially appears that his relationship with Shamash may satisfy this need, Shamash tells him to snap out of it, saying, "It is your wrong thoughts that must change," and steers him to meeting Gilgamesh in a spirit of friendship. While forces beyond the control of either Enkidu or Gilgamesh engineer this friendship, it appears that while Enkidu truly seeks a meeting of the heart, Gilgamesh merely needs someone to tone down his aggressive impulses.

This inconsistency between the roles of Enkidu and Gilgamesh is repeated in other parts of the text. For example, while Gilgamesh's enthusiasm to journey and destroy the great Cedar Forest is particularly palpable (Kovacs 20-21), Enkidu is less sanguine. Worriedly, he appeals to the Elders, requesting them to "say to him [Gilgamesh] that he must not go to the Cedar Forest - the journey is not to be made" (Kovacs 20). Here, Enkidu is looking after his friend, while Gilgamesh is primarily after a new adventure. The reasons for this disparity are made clear in the next tablet. While Gilgamesh does not relent, Enkidu's role in this journey is clarified in the next table. The Elders advise Gilgamesh not to rely upon his "vast strength' but instead upon Enkidu. They urge him to "let Enkidu go ahead of you... Enkidu will protect the friend, will keep the comrade safe". According to the Elders, Enkidu's role is protecting Gilgamesh. This is consistent with the role initially assigned to Enkidu by the gods at the outset. Curiously, Gilgamesh has no such responsibility towards Enkidu. Despite Enkidu's entreaty, "My Friend, turn back!" (Kovacs 28), Gilgamesh persists in undertaking the perilous journey because the Elders have assured him that "Enkidu will protect the friend" (Kovacs 28).

Gilgamesh does appear to have a brief moment in which considers acting on behalf of Enkidu, but this moment is fleeting. Just before he is slain, Humbaba prophesizes Enkido's early death, saying "he will not live the longer of the two" (Kovacs 28). Apparently, this gives Gilgamesh pause because Enkidu angrily asserts that "my friend, I have been talking to you but you have not been listening to me. You have been listening to the curse of Humbaba!" Although the meaning is not entirely clear, it appears that Enkidu does not consider this threat a meaningful one, whereas Gilgamesh, who is charged with having superior knowledge, is fully aware of the danger. Despite this awareness, Gilgamesh quickly overcomes his reluctance to sacrifice Enkidu.

The foregoing evidence forces the reader to conclude that despite the many claims of friendship between Enkidu and Gilgamesh which pepper the text, this is not a friendship as understood in modern times. Enkidu's repeated and endearing acts of loyalty and friendship are never reciprocated in a meaningful way during his lifetime. This disparity in roles may be attributed to the parties having been placed on an uneven footing by the gods at the outset. Alternatively, it may reflect a relationship between one who was two-thirds god and one who was wholly mortal. Regardless of the reason, however, it is perplexing that true friendship remains beyond the reach of one described as "awesome to perfection" (Kovacs 4).

Works Cited

Kovacs, Maureen Gallery, trans. The Epic of Gilgamesh. Stanford, CA: Stanford University Press, 1989

Essay: Enkidu's Deathbed Realization

# Essay: Power Relations in Doctor Faustus

**by Gena Archer**
**April 22, 2007**

The play Doctor Faustus is about a Doctor called Faustus who sells his soul to the devil in order to obtain honor, wealth and magical powers. He is a powerless individual, who periodically gains a false sense of power through the prospects of wealth and honor.

Mephistophilis and the devil have an enormous amount of power over Faustus, because they possess what he desires, that is, power. He craves to have power so desperately that he ends up selling his soul to the devil. The two angles in the first scene of the play also have power over Faustus. Apart from external forces, Faustus also finds himself powerless when it comes to his mind, which is, unstable and takes him in many different directions. Though out the play power relations are being established. This can be seen through the various settings of the play such as lighting, character placement and costumes.

In the first scene Faustus enters his study. In the study there is a desk and chair in the corner, a shelf of books and a very dim light that hangs from the ceiling. He is pacing up and down the length of the room. While pacing he is contemplating the pro and con of giving his soul to god or the devil. Faustus' pacing motions in this scene represents him wavering in thought;thus, his inability to master his mind. This causes his mind to have power over him leading him into many directions he should follow in making his decision. At one point his mind say, " Despair in God and trust in Belzebub!" (5), and at another it suggests, " Adjure this magic, turn to God again". This battle in his mind takes control over him making him unstable physically and mentally. Since light is considered to be powerful when it is bright, the dim light in the room reflects his powerlessness.

While contemplation two angles appear unto Faustus, and he falls on his knees as a sign of submission. The angles stand on opposite side of him as he remains on his knees. This stage setting shows that these Angels have influence and power over him. His position shows inferiority and the Angels stand in power and Authority. These angles, one good and the other evil, tries to influence him into following their advice. The good angel says, "sweet Faustus, think of heaven and heavenly things," and the bad angel says, "No, Faustus think of honor and of wealth." This statement that the bad angel makes captures Fautus' attention, because it addresses his inner most desires. He desires to be powerful, to be rich and to have prestige. Because the bad angel gets the last word and is the last to leave this scene, it shows that the bad angel has more power over Faustus than the good angel.

The room becomes fully lit and Faustus takes center stage. This time he is not pacing up and down the stage; he stands firmly on the grown giving a few hand gestures. The staging, including the bright light and fix posture, shows that Faustus gains a sense of power in the play. He is no longer wavering in his thoughts, and he has made up his mind as to what step he is going to take in his decision making process. However, this power is not real. He is giving a false sense of power through the prospects of wealth and honor the devil promises him. It is false power, because he gains nothing that he desires, such as wealth, honor and magic. It is merely the idea of having these things that gives him personal power and confidence, he says: "What power can hurt me? Faustus, thou art safe." (26).

Mephistophilis enters the scene. He is a tall figure, and he has on a long black robe. Faustus is still at the center of the stage, as Mephistophilis begins to circles him periodically. This circular motion represents entrapment. It further shows that he is in control; thus, he has power over Faustus. He has power over Faustus because he possesses what he desires to have, that is, wealth and honor. Mephilistophilis is aware of what Faustus wants; thus, he tries to manipulate him with wealth and honor in order to gain his soul. To do this Melphistophilis treacherously submits himself to Faustus by going on his knees. He does this to give Faustus a false sense of power and superiority. He says, "That I shall wait on Faustus whilst he lives, so he will buy my service with his soul" (33). It is important to note that the real power does not shift. Mephistophilis is still in control as he continues to manupulate Faustus. In an aside he states, "what will I not do in order to obtain his soul!"(74)

In the second scene Faustus is sitting at his desk with a razer in his hand. It is at this point that he is about to sign over his soul to the devil with his blood. His blood freezes and Mephistophilis exits the scene to bring him fire to dissolve it. Faustus on stage position of him sitting and Mephistophilis is standing, further shows Mephistophilis' power over him. It is at this point that Faustus' false sense of power begins to disappear, as he once again begins to waver in his decision, he says: " what might the staying of my blood protend? Is it unwilling that I write this bill?" (66). As Faust begins to loose his false power; "to delight his mind" Mephistophilis send in devils to give him crowns and rich appeals. The costumes of rich apparels given to Faustus signify royalty and riches that gives Faustus a false sense of power one again.

Faustus has no real power in the play. Mephistophilis and the Devil have an enormous amount of power over him. They are able to manipulate him into giving his soul. In doing so they use power making Fautus feel as though he is in control when he really isn't. Thus, though out the play he gains power, but it is not genuine. He often goes back into a state of powerlessness, which is only dependent on the prospects of wealth and power. These power relations can be seen though out the staging of the play. Whenever Faustus feels powerful the setting changes the lights are bright and he stands firmly center stage; however, when the real powerful characters, such as, the angles and Mephistophilis enters the scene the setting shifts. On these occasions Faustus becomes inferior and submissive, which can be seen though his stage placement in relation to the other characters.

# Quiz 1

1. **What kind of king is Gilgamesh? How is he first described to us?**
   A. A tyrant who oppresses his people
   B. A wise sage who rules with fairness
   C. A holy man who consults the gods
   D. A fierce warrior who protects his city

2. **Why did the gods create Enkidu?**
   A. To defeat and overthrow Gilgamesh
   B. To prevent Gilgamesh from destroying them
   C. To stop Gilgamesh from finding a bride
   D. To be a counterforce to Gilgamesh

3. **What did the trapper do after first seeing Enkidu?**
   A. Started a fire to drive the creature away
   B. Set larger traps to catch this beast
   C. Told his father he had seen a giant man
   D. Warned the people in the village of a monster

4. **How did the animals react to Enkidu after he was visited by Shamhat, the temple prostitute?**
   A. Attacked him and drove him into the woods
   B. Appointed him as their protector from hunters
   C. Asked him to lead them to find food and water
   D. Rejected him and no longer regarded him as kin

5. **What objects are featured in Gilgamesh's dreams prior to meeting Enkidu?**
   A. A bull and a cart
   B. A meteor and an axe
   C. A sword and a shield
   D. A mountain and a lion

6. **What was Gilgamesh doing that angered Enkidu to challenge him to a fight?**
   A. Enslaving peasants for his own amusement
   B. Sleeping with newly married brides
   C. Collecting heavy taxes from farmers
   D. Putting the elderly of the city to death

7. **What did Enkidu do after losing a fight with Gilgamesh?**
   A. Acknowledged his greater strength
   B. Returned in shame to the wilderness
   C. Agreed to become his personal servant
   D. Begged him to spare his life

8. **What did Gilgamesh propose that he and Enkidu do to gain fame and recognition?**
   A. Cross the Euphrates to conquer Shurrupak
   B. Climb the mountains of Mashu to find Shamhat
   C. Journey to the Cedar Forest to defeat Humbaba
   D. Liberate Mesopotamia from the rule of Ea

9. **What did Ninsun do before Gilgamesh and Enkidu left on their quest?**
   A. Told them a cautionary tale
   B. Prayed for their safety
   C. Obtained weapons for use
   D. Packed food for them

10. **Gilgamesh dreams of a mountainslide and a fiery storm. What does Enkidu tell him these dreams have predicted?**
    A. That they must return to the city quickly
    B. That they will encounter terrible weather
    C. That they will be victorious in their quest
    D. That they should choose another path

11. **What did Gilgamesh and Enkidu do upon hearing Humbaba's bellowing in the forest?**
    A. Called him out to face them in battle
    B. Encouraged each other not to be afraid
    C. Hid behind some bushes until he passed
    D. Mimicked his voice to confuse him

12. **What did Shamhash do to Humbaba to aid Gilgamesh and Enkidu?**
    A. Bound him with thirteen winds
    B. Fed him four herbs to poison his heart
    C. Told his seven disciples to block out the sun
    D. Summoned ten birds to peck out his eyes

13. **What did Humbaba do before he was beheaded?**
    A. Pleaded with Enlil for assistance
    B. Cursed Gilgamesh and Enkidu
    C. Said a prayer to Anu for forgiveness
    D. Gave Ishtar instructions in the event of his death

14. **What did Gilgamesh and Enkidu plan to do with a giant cedar tree they cut down after defeating Humbaba?**
    A. Construct a new home in the forest
    B. Fashion weapons for their next adventure
    C. Use it to build a gate for a temple
    D. Carve an idol as homage to the gods

15. **Why did Gilgamesh reject the Goddess Ishtar?**
    A. Because he wished to take a vow of celibacy
    B. Because he knew how she treated other lovers
    C. Because he had already selected another woman
    D. Because he wanted to focus on starting a family

16. **What did Ishtar do after being rejected by Gilgamesh?**
    A. Sought romantic advice from Utnapishtim
    B. Asked Anu to punish him immediately
    C. Visited Shamhash to acquire poison
    D. Threatened to make Ninsun very sick

17. **What did the Bull of Heaven do to the city of Uruk?**
    A. Destroyed the temple walls
    B. Trampled all the city's crops
    C. Brought about a drought
    D. Unleashed a deadly plague

18. **How did Enkidu further enrage Ishtar after he and Gilgamesh slayed the Bull of Heaven?**
    A. Threw its hindquarters at her face
    B. Destroyed a temple built in her name
    C. Convinced the other gods to shun her
    D. Told her she was too ugly to be a goddess

19. **What did Enkidu do after he fell ill?**
    A. Beseeched Urshanabi for a cure
    B. Cursed Shamhat and the trapper
    C. Blamed Gilgamesh and his mother
    D. Insulted Enlil and the other gods

20. **What was Enkidu's final lament before he died?**
    A. He wished to become the king of his own city
    B. He wanted to travel and see the world
    C. He wanted to die a heroic death in battle
    D. He wished he could have started a family

21. **Prior to his death Enkidu has a dream in which he is taken to the underworld. How does he describe the underworld to Gilgamesh?**
    A. A house of dust
    B. A land of despair
    C. A valley of decay
    D. A kingdom of grief

22. **Gilgamesh mourns over Enkidu's body for six days and seven nights. What finally prompts him to bury his friend?**
    A. A worm crawls out of his nose
    B. A jackal comes to claim the body
    C. The stench of decay becomes too strong
    D. His skin turns black and falls off

23. **As Tablet Nine begins, Gilgamesh is mourning the loss of Enkidu. How does the text describe him?**
    A. Roaming the wilderness dressed in animal skins
    B. Seeking out battles in a full suit of armor
    C. Walking the streets of his city completely naked
    D. Locked in his chambers adorned in fine attire

24. **What did Gilgamesh decide to do after Enkidu's death?**
    A. Relinquish his throne and live in the wild
    B. Take his own life to end his suffering
    C. Challenge the gods to battle him in war
    D. Learn about the secret of immortality

25. **What did Gilgamesh do when he arrived at the mountains of Mashu?**
    A. Encountered two terrifying scorpion-men
    B. Questioned a deformed hermit for directions
    C. Wrestled a sacred lion with giant teeth
    D. Climbed it to drink from a magic fountain

# Quiz 1 Answer Key

1. **(A)** A tyrant who oppresses his people
2. **(D)** To be a counterforce to Gilgamesh
3. **(C)** Told his father he had seen a giant man
4. **(D)** Rejected him and no longer regarded him as kin
5. **(B)** A meteor and an axe
6. **(B)** Sleeping with newly married brides
7. **(A)** Acknowledged his greater strength
8. **(C)** Journey to the Cedar Forest to defeat Humbaba
9. **(B)** Prayed for their safety
10. **(C)** That they will be victorious in their quest
11. **(B)** Encouraged each other not to be afraid
12. **(A)** Bound him with thirteen winds
13. **(B)** Cursed Gilgamesh and Enkidu
14. **(C)** Use it to build a gate for a temple
15. **(B)** Because he knew how she treated other lovers
16. **(B)** Asked Anu to punish him immediately
17. **(C)** Brought about a drought
18. **(A)** Threw its hindquarters at her face
19. **(B)** Cursed Shamhat and the trapper
20. **(C)** He wanted to die a heroic death in battle
21. **(A)** A house of dust
22. **(A)** A worm crawls out of his nose
23. **(A)** Roaming the wilderness dressed in animal skins
24. **(D)** Learn about the secret of immortality
25. **(A)** Encountered two terrifying scorpion-men

# Quiz 2

1. **What did Gilgamesh encounter upon entering the gate leading through the mountains of Mashu?**
    A. Complete darkness that hindered his way
    B. A thick choking smoke that burned his eyes
    C. A collapsed mine that blocked his path
    D. Fierce creatures who clawed at his flesh

2. **What did Siduri do upon first meeting Gilgamesh?**
    A. Drove him from her home with a sword
    B. Challenged him to solve a difficult riddle
    C. Instructed him to cross a dangerous bridge
    D. Discouraged him from continuing his quest

3. **What is Siduri's profession?**
    A. Alewife
    B. Priestess
    C. Maid
    D. Prostitute

4. **What did Gilgamesh do upon meeting Urshanabi, the ferryman?**
    A. Killed the stone giants who accompanied him
    B. Caught a giant fish that lived in the sea
    C. Wrestled an ogre who emerged from a cave
    D. Snared a winged horse to fly over the sea

5. **What does Urshanabi tell Gilgamesh to do in order to cross Hubur, the waters of death?**
    A. Cut down trees to use as oars
    B. Build a raft from wood and clay
    C. Build a bridge from giant stones
    D. Swing across on a long rope

6. **What does Gilgamesh first notice about Utnapishtim upon meeting him?**
    A. He is decrepit and very weak
    B. He is alone and terribly lonely
    C. He is youthful and strong
    D. He is no different from him

7. **What does Utnapishtim tell Gilgamesh when Gilgamesh tells him the story of his grief?**
   A. Death must be accepted as inevitable
   B. Immortality is an endless prison sentence
   C. Mourning the loss of life is selfish and pointless
   D. A legacy of fame is the best thing in life

8. **What city did Utnapishtim mention in the flood story he told Gilgamesh?**
   A. Nippur
   B. Shurrupak
   C. Kish
   D. Uruk

9. **What did Utnapishtim say the gods instructed him to do in his story about the great flood?**
   A. Warn his people so that they may flee in time
   B. Take his family to the highest mountaintop
   C. Sacrifice a lamb to avert a terrible disaster
   D. Build a boat and stock it with all animals

10. **How long does Utnapishtim say the storm that brought the flood lasted?**
    A. An entire year
    B. An entire month
    C. Fourty days and nights
    D. Six days and seven nights

11. **What did Utnapishtim say Ishtar did after the flood?**
    A. Introduced new species all over the land
    B. Drained the waters back to begin life anew
    C. Grieved over the death of humanity
    D. Began a divine war with the other gods

12. **What did Enlil do after Ea reprimanded him for the flood?**
    A. Granted Utnapishtim and his wife greath wealth
    B. Granted Utnapishtim and his wife a kingdom
    C. Granted Utnapishtim and his wife a baby son
    D. Granted Utnapishtim and his wife immortality

13. **What challenge does Utnapishtim issue to Gilgamesh?**
    A. To go a year without human contact
    B. To go a month without speaking
    C. To go a week without food
    D. To go a week without sleep

14. **Why did Utnapishtim's wife bake a loaf of bread each day?**
    A. To convince the gods to protect Gilgamesh
    B. To prove that Gilgamesh had slept that long
    C. To satiate Gilgamesh's immense hunger
    D. To feed Gilgamesh on his return trip home

15. **Utnapishtim tells Gilgamesh of a magic plant. Where does he say this plant is located?**
    A. On the peak of the tallest mountain
    B. At the bottom of the ocean
    C. On a hillside protected by lions
    D. In a valley inhabited by a monster

16. **How did Gilgamesh lose the magic plant?**
    A. A woman he meets takes it while he is asleep
    B. He drops it down a dark hole while he is drunk
    C. A bird swooped down and took it from his hands
    D. A serpent stole it while he was bathing

17. **What did Gilgamesh do when he returned to Uruk with Urshanabi?**
    A. Ordered a great feast to be prepared in his honor
    B. Took him to see the city elders and tell his story
    C. Asked him to stay and help him rule the city
    D. Showed him the city walls and its temple

18. **Why did the Elders advise Gilgamesh to let Enkidu lead him to the Cedar Forest?**
    A. He had knowledge of the wilderness
    B. He knew how to open the gate that blocked it
    C. He had been to the forest once before
    D. He knew a secret short cut to get there

19. **What remarkable physical feat do Gilgamesh and Enkidu perform on their way to the Cedar Forest?**
    A. They trick the gods and steal the secret power of flight
    B. They tame a herd of crazed wild horses and ride them
    C. They complete a journey of weeks in a matter of days
    D. They swim across whole oceans each on a single breath

20. **What did Ishtar threaten to do if Anu did not release the Bull of Heaven?**
    A. Open the doors of the underworld and free the dead
    B. Destroy all the crops with a horde of locusts
    C. Summon a great storm to punish all of humanity
    D. Cover the land in fire with an erupting volcano

21. **What did Gilgamesh do with the horns of the Bull of Heaven?**
    A. Sharpened the tips to create a new weapon
    B. Attached them to a fierce helmet he commissioned
    C. Hung them in his chambers as a trophy
    D. Fashioned a medal to wear around his neck

22. **What happened in a dream Enkidu had after he and Gilgamesh had defeated the Bull of Heaven?**
    A. Ishtar came in the night to kill them as they slept
    B. Uruk was destroyed in a terrible all-consuming fire
    C. Anu and the other gods were meeting in council
    D. Enlil commanded them to make an offering to him

23. **Who did Gilgamesh command to mourn Enkidu after his death?**
    A. The animals, mountains, and grasslands
    B. The demons who live in and protect the forests
    C. The gods in heaven and the accursed in the netherworld
    D. The great fish that swim in the abyss beneath the earth

24. **What did Utnapishtim do after seven days in the boat he had built?**
    A. Moved the lions to another deck so they wouldn't eat other animals
    B. Rode atop a giant fish and saw the destruction
    C. Made a ritual sacrifice in a desperate plea to the gods
    D. Freed birds to see if they would find land

25. **What did Utnapishtim do after finally going ashore after the Flood?**
    A. Sang a song to memorialize the dead
    B. Cursed the gods for their arrogance
    C. Sacrificed a lamb upon an altar
    D. Burned down the ark he had built

# Quiz 2 Answer Key

1. **(A)** Complete darkness that hindered his way
2. **(D)** Discouraged him from continuing his quest
3. **(A)** Alewife
4. **(A)** Killed the stone giants who accompanied him
5. **(A)** Cut down trees to use as oars
6. **(D)** He is no different from him
7. **(A)** Death must be accepted as inevitable
8. **(B)** Shurrupak
9. **(D)** Build a boat and stock it with all animals
10. **(D)** Six days and seven nights
11. **(C)** Grieved over the death of humanity
12. **(D)** Granted Utnapishtim and his wife immortality
13. **(D)** To go a week without sleep
14. **(B)** To prove that Gilgamesh had slept that long
15. **(B)** At the bottom of the ocean
16. **(D)** A serpent stole it while he was bathing
17. **(D)** Showed him the city walls and its temple
18. **(A)** He had knowledge of the wilderness
19. **(C)** They complete a journey of weeks in a matter of days
20. **(A)** Open the doors of the underworld and free the dead
21. **(C)** Hung them in his chambers as a trophy
22. **(C)** Anu and the other gods were meeting in council
23. **(A)** The animals, mountains, and grasslands
24. **(D)** Freed birds to see if they would find land
25. **(C)** Sacrificed a lamb upon an altar

# Quiz 3

1. **Where does Siduri say Gilgamesh can find Urshanabi?**
   A. Atop a mountain
   B. On an island
   C. Inside a cave
   D. The bottom of the sea

2. **What did Gilgamesh do after Enkidu passed away?**
   A. Drank excessively and fought a demon
   B. Took spiritual vows and lived in the forest
   C. Swore to avenge the death of his friend
   D. Tore his clothes and wore animal skins

3. **What is the wedge-shaped writing in which the poem is written called?**
   A. Aramaic
   B. Hieroglyphics
   C. Katakana
   D. Cuneiform

4. **What are the tablets on which the story is recorded made of?**
   A. Bronze
   B. Clay
   C. Wood
   D. Stone

5. **What did Utnapishtim say Enlil did after the flood had subsided?**
   A. Set the sky ablaze so it rained fire
   B. Wrought a terrible pestilence on the land
   C. Granted he and his wife immortality
   D. Brought all the dead back to life

6. **Where did Enkidu have his first taste of cooked food and beer?**
   A. On a battlefield
   B. A shepherd's camp
   C. The royal palace
   D. A tavern in the city

7. **Utnapishtim was the king of what city?**
    A. Shurrupak
    B. Uruk
    C. Cairo
    D. Mesopotamia

8. **Shamhat is a temple prostitute in whose temple?**
    A. Enlil's
    B. Ishtar's
    C. Shamash's
    D. Sin's

9. **What type of trees made up the forest guarded by Humbaba?**
    A. Cherry
    B. Oak
    C. Pine
    D. Cedar

10. **Whom does Humbaba serve?**
    A. Ishtar
    B. Ea
    C. Enlil
    D. Utnapishtim

11. **Whom did Gilgamesh ask for help in midst of battle with Humbaba?**
    A. Enkidu
    B. Ninsun
    C. Shamash
    D. Anu

12. **What is Urshanabi's profession?**
    A. Priest
    B. Boatman
    C. Shepherd
    D. Craftsman

13. **What did Utnapishtim instruct Urshanabi to do with Gilgamesh?**
    A. Help him journey to convene with the gods
    B. Accompany him back to his home
    C. Instruct him to write down his story
    D. Take him to the underworld

14. **What did Ishtar promise to give Gilgamesh if he became her lover?**
    A. A shield adorned with jewels
    B. A chariot of lapis lazuli
    C. An indestructible sword
    D. A temple made of gold

15. **Who are Ishtar's parents?**
    A. Siduri and Urshanabi
    B. Enlil and Ea
    C. Anu and Antum
    D. Shamash and Shamhat

16. **Who are Gilgamesh's parents?**
    A. Sin and Ishtar
    B. Ninsun and Lugalbanda
    C. Ninsun and Enlil
    D. Shamash and Antum

17. **On the shores of what river did Utnapishtim say Shurrupak sat?**
    A. Tigris
    B. Euphrates
    C. Nile
    D. Blue

18. **Which of the following physical characteristics did Enkidu exhibit when he was spotted by the trapper?**
    A. Body hair
    B. Horns
    C. Glowing eyes
    D. Sharp talons

19. **To whom did Gilgamesh make an offering with the horns of the Bull of Heaven?**
    A. Ninsun
    B. Ea
    C. Lugulbanda
    D. Enlil

20. **Who does the text say Enkidu runs and feeds with at the beginning of the epic?**
    A. Wolves
    B. Gazelles
    C. Elephants
    D. Bears

21. **What kind of animals did Gilgamesh pray to Sin, the moon god, to protect him from?**
    A. Tigers
    B. Wolves
    C. Jackals
    D. Lions

22. **Ereshkigal is queen of what domain?**
    A. The city of Uruk
    B. The Cedar Forest
    C. The Nether World
    D. The Seven Seas

23. **How long did it take the people of Shuruppak to construct the boat for Utnapishtim?**
    A. One month
    B. Seven days
    C. Forty days
    D. A fortnight

24. **Gilgamesh instructs the craftsmen to make a statue of Enkidu after his death. What is this statue to be made of?**
    A. Obsidian
    B. Gold
    C. Lapis Lazuli
    D. Marble

25. **Who created Enkidu?**
     A. Shamash
     B. Ea
     C. Enlil
     D. Aruru

# Quiz 3 Answer Key

1. **(B)** On an island
2. **(D)** Tore his clothes and wore animal skins
3. **(D)** Cuneiform
4. **(B)** Clay
5. **(C)** Granted he and his wife immortality
6. **(B)** A shepherd's camp
7. **(A)** Shurrupak
8. **(B)** Ishtar's
9. **(D)** Cedar
10. **(C)** Enlil
11. **(C)** Shamash
12. **(B)** Boatman
13. **(B)** Accompany him back to his home
14. **(B)** A chariot of lapis lazuli
15. **(C)** Anu and Antum
16. **(B)** Ninsun and Lugalbanda
17. **(B)** Euphrates
18. **(A)** Body hair
19. **(C)** Lugulbanda
20. **(B)** Gazelles
21. **(D)** Lions
22. **(C)** The Nether World
23. **(B)** Seven days
24. **(B)** Gold
25. **(D)** Aruru

# Quiz 4

1. Who is the editor credited with compiling the most complete version of the epic?
   A. Sin-leqi-Unnini
   B. Urshanabi
   C. Atrahasis
   D. Utnapishtim

2. What did Urshanabi warn Gilgamesh not to do while they were sailing to find Utnapishtim?
   A. Fish for food in the sea
   B. Touch the deadly waters
   C. Stare at his own reflection in the water
   D. Drink the water around him

3. What did Gilgamesh do with his animal skin when his punting poles aboard Urshanabi's boat were all used up?
   A. Used it as a net to catch a fish
   B. Shielded them from the hot sun
   C. Made an offering to the wind god
   D. Held it up as an improvised sail

4. Who did Ninsun adopt as her son?
   A. Enkidu
   B. Gilgamesh
   C. Urshanabi
   D. Utnapishtim

5. What was the profession of Puzuramurri, the man Utnapishtim turns his house over to before the Flood?
   A. Farmer
   B. Priest
   C. Caulker
   D. Carpenter

6. What object does Gilgamesh drop into the Nether World in Tablet XII?
   A. A stringed lute
   B. A fine robe
   C. A drumstick
   D. A mask

7. **What can the magic plant that Utnapishtim tells Gilgamesh about do?**
   A. Restore an elderly person's youth
   B. Turn any stone into pure gold
   C. Imbue its holder with great strength
   D. Grant its owner supreme wisdom

8. **Who tells Enlil that the 'punishment should always fit the crime'?**
   A. Ishtar
   B. Ea
   C. Anu
   D. Aruru

9. **Ishtar tells Utnapishtim that she wears a necklace to remind her of the consequences of the Flood. Of what is this necklace made?**
   A. Copper
   B. Platinum
   C. Gold
   D. Lapis Lazuli

10. **What other name does the text give to Gilgamesh?**
    A. Wise Eagle
    B. Great Lion
    C. Savage Wolf
    D. Wild Ox

11. **What did Enkidu realize he wanted after his encounter with Shamhat?**
    A. A family
    B. A companion
    C. A home
    D. A child

12. **What did Shamhat do to clothe Enkidu?**
    A. Divided her own robes
    B. Summoned a city tailor
    C. Sacrificed an animal for its skin
    D. Borrowed the tunic of a shepherd

13. **What did Enkidu do to protect the shepherd's camp?**
    A. Fought off a band of savage thieves
    B. Built a fence using the trees of the forest
    C. Took night watch to guard them from animals
    D. Killed a demon that fed on their flocks

14. **What is another name that the text uses for Gilgamesh's mother, Ninsun?**
    A. River Goddess
    B. She-Wolf
    C. Queen Lionness
    D. Lady Wildcow

15. **What did the heroes do before leaving Uruk to face Humbaba?**
    A. Trained an army to guard the city in their absence
    B. Visited the armor makers to obtain weapons
    C. Visited a god to receive a protective blessing
    D. Wrestled a hundred men to toughen their bodies

16. **What type of grain does Gilgamesh offer Shamash before he and Enkidu face Humbaba?**
    A. Barley
    B. Corn
    C. Wheat
    D. Flour

17. **How does Enkidu interpret the dreams Gilgamesh has before they face Humbaba?**
    A. They are a testament to their friendship
    B. They are a warning from the gods
    C. They foretell of an unseen consequence
    D. They are favorable and fortunate

18. **How many garments make up the terrors of Humbaba?**
    A. Ten
    B. Five
    C. Three
    D. Seven

19. **How did Enkidu and Gilgamesh return to Uruk after defeating Humbaba?**
    A. They built a raft and sailed
    B. Captured a giant winged bird
    C. Traveled with an army from Uruk
    D. Tamed and rode two wild stallions

20. **The original versions of the epic appear in several different languages. Which of the following is not one of them?**
    A. Akkadian
    B. Sumerian
    C. Babylonian
    D. Arabic

21. **What is the distinguishing characteristic of Mount Mashu's peak?**
    A. Smoke billows from it
    B. It has twin peaks
    C. It is where the moon rises
    D. It is always covered in fog

22. **Scholars say that Mount Nisir in Utnapishtim's flood account is a comparable to what mountain in the Bible?**
    A. Mount Everest
    B. Mount Damavand
    C. Mount Kilimanjaro
    D. Mount Ararat

23. **What is the name of the magical plant that Utnapishtim describes?**
    A. How-The-Old-Man-Once-Again-Becomes-A-Young-Man
    B. How-The-Young-Man-Gains-The-Wisdom-Of-An-Old-Man
    C. How-The-Young-Man-Lives-Forever
    D. How-The-Old-Man-Becomes-A-God

24. **Who did Ishtar say was forbidden from attending Utnapishtim's sacrificial offering following the Flood?**
    A. Enkidu
    B. Ninurta
    C. Ea
    D. Enlil

25. **What did Ea do to warn Utnapishtim of the coming flood?**
    A. Whispered to him through his house walls
    B. Took the form of a priest in the temple
    C. Appeared to him in a clairvoyant dream
    D. Transformed into a singing nightingale and woke him

# Quiz 4 Answer Key

1. (**A**) Sin-leqi-Unnini
2. (**B**) Touch the deadly waters
3. (**D**) Held it up as an improvised sail
4. (**A**) Enkidu
5. (**C**) Caulker
6. (**C**) A drumstick
7. (**A**) Restore an elderly person's youth
8. (**B**) Ea
9. (**D**) Lapis Lazuli
10. (**D**) Wild Ox
11. (**B**) A companion
12. (**A**) Divided her own robes
13. (**C**) Took night watch to guard them from animals
14. (**D**) Lady Wildcow
15. (**B**) Visited the armor makers to obtain weapons
16. (**D**) Flour
17. (**D**) They are favorable and fortunate
18. (**D**) Seven
19. (**A**) They built a raft and sailed
20. (**D**) Arabic
21. (**B**) It has twin peaks
22. (**D**) Mount Ararat
23. (**A**) How-The-Old-Man-Once-Again-Becomes-A-Young-Man
24. (**D**) Enlil
25. (**A**) Whispered to him through his house walls

# ClassicNotes

# GrⱯdeSaver™

*Getting you the grade since 1999*™

## Other ClassicNotes from GradeSaver™

1984
Absalom, Absalom
Adam Bede
The Adventures of Augie
  March
The Adventures of
  Huckleberry Finn
The Adventures of Tom
  Sawyer
The Aeneid
Agamemnon
The Age of Innocence
The Alchemist (Coelho)
The Alchemist (Jonson)
Alice in Wonderland
All My Sons
All Quiet on the Western
  Front
All the King's Men
All the Pretty Horses
Allen Ginsberg's Poetry
The Ambassadors
American Beauty
And Then There Were
  None
Angela's Ashes
Animal Farm
Anna Karenina
Anthem
Antigone
Antony and Cleopatra
Aristotle's Ethics
Aristotle's Poetics
Aristotle's Politics
As I Lay Dying
As You Like It

Astrophil and Stella
Atlas Shrugged
Atonement
The Awakening
Babbitt
The Bacchae
Bartleby the Scrivener
The Bean Trees
The Bell Jar
Beloved
Benito Cereno
Beowulf
Bhagavad-Gita
Billy Budd
Black Boy
Bleak House
Bless Me, Ultima
Blindness
Blood Wedding
The Bloody Chamber
Bluest Eye
The Bonfire of the
  Vanities
The Book of the Duchess
  and Other Poems
The Book Thief
Brave New World
Breakfast at Tiffany's
Breakfast of Champions
The Brief Wondrous Life
  of Oscar Wao
The Brothers Karamazov
The Burning Plain and
  Other Stories
A Burnt-Out Case
By Night in Chile

Call of the Wild
Candide
The Canterbury Tales
Cat on a Hot Tin Roof
Cat's Cradle
Catch-22
The Catcher in the Rye
The Caucasian Chalk
  Circle
Charlotte's Web
The Cherry Orchard
The Chocolate War
The Chosen
A Christmas Carol
Christopher Marlowe's
  Poems
Chronicle of a Death
  Foretold
Civil Disobedience
Civilization and Its
  Discontents
A Clockwork Orange
Coleridge's Poems
The Color of Water
The Color Purple
Comedy of Errors
Communist Manifesto
A Confederacy of
  Dunces
Confessions
Connecticut Yankee in
  King Arthur's Court
The Consolation of
  Philosophy
Coriolanus

For our full list of over 250 Study Guides, Quizzes,
Sample College Application Essays, Literature Essays and E-texts, visit:

**www.gradesaver.com**

# ClassicNotes

# GradeSaver™

*Getting you the grade since 1999*™

## Other ClassicNotes from GradeSaver™

The Count of Monte Cristo
The Country Wife
Crime and Punishment
The Crucible
Cry, the Beloved Country
The Crying of Lot 49
The Curious Incident of the Dog in the Night-time
Cymbeline
Daisy Miller
David Copperfield
Death in Venice
Death of a Salesman
The Death of Ivan Ilych
Democracy in America
Devil in a Blue Dress
Dharma Bums
The Diary of a Young Girl by Anne Frank
Disgrace
Divine Comedy-I: Inferno
Do Androids Dream of Electric Sheep?
Doctor Faustus (Marlowe)
A Doll's House
Don Quixote Book I
Don Quixote Book II
Dora: An Analysis of a Case of Hysteria
Dr. Jekyll and Mr. Hyde
Dracula

Dubliners
East of Eden
Electra by Sophocles
The Electric Kool-Aid Acid Test
Emily Dickinson's Collected Poems
Emma
Ender's Game
Endgame
The English Patient
The Epic of Gilgamesh
Ethan Frome
The Eumenides
Everyman: Morality Play
Everything is Illuminated
The Faerie Queene
Fahrenheit 451
The Fall of the House of Usher
A Farewell to Arms
The Federalist Papers
Fences
Flags of Our Fathers
Flannery O'Connor's Stories
For Whom the Bell Tolls
The Fountainhead
Frankenstein
Franny and Zooey
The Giver
The Glass Castle
The Glass Menagerie
The God of Small Things
Goethe's Faust
The Good Earth

The Grapes of Wrath
Great Expectations
The Great Gatsby
Grendel
The Guest
Gulliver's Travels
Hamlet
The Handmaid's Tale
Hard Times
Haroun and the Sea of Stories
Harry Potter and the Philosopher's Stone
Heart of Darkness
Hedda Gabler
Henry IV (Pirandello)
Henry IV Part 1
Henry IV Part 2
Henry V
Herzog
Hippolytus
The Hobbit
Homo Faber
House of Mirth
The House of the Seven Gables
The House of the Spirits
House on Mango Street
How the Garcia Girls Lost Their Accents
Howards End
A Hunger Artist
I Know Why the Caged Bird Sings
I, Claudius
An Ideal Husband

For our full list of over 250 Study Guides, Quizzes,
Sample College Application Essays, Literature Essays and E-texts, visit:

**www.gradesaver.com**

# ClassicNotes

# GrAdeSaver™

*Getting you the grade since 1999*™

## Other ClassicNotes from GradeSaver™

Iliad
The Importance of Being
  Earnest
In Cold Blood
In Our Time
In the Time of the
  Butterflies
Inherit the Wind
An Inspector Calls
Into the Wild
Invisible Man
The Island of Dr. Moreau
Jane Eyre
Jazz
The Jew of Malta
Joseph Andrews
The Joy Luck Club
Julius Caesar
The Jungle
Jungle of Cities
Kama Sutra
Kate Chopin's Short
  Stories
Kidnapped
King Lear
King Solomon's Mines
The Kite Runner
Last of the Mohicans
Leaves of Grass
The Legend of Sleepy
  Hollow
A Lesson Before Dying
Leviathan
Libation Bearers
Life is Beautiful
Life of Pi

Light In August
Like Water for Chocolate
The Lion, the Witch and
  the Wardrobe
Little Women
Lolita
Long Day's Journey Into
  Night
Look Back in Anger
Lord Jim
Lord of the Flies
The Lord of the Rings:
  The Fellowship of the
  Ring
The Lord of the Rings:
  The Return of the
  King
The Lord of the Rings:
  The Two Towers
A Lost Lady
The Lottery and Other
  Stories
Love in the Time of
  Cholera
The Love Song of J.
  Alfred Prufrock
The Lovely Bones
Lucy
Macbeth
Madame Bovary
Maggie: A Girl of the
  Streets and Other
  Stories
Manhattan Transfer
Mankind: Medieval
  Morality Plays

Mansfield Park
The Marrow of Tradition
The Master and
  Margarita
MAUS
The Mayor of
  Casterbridge
Measure for Measure
Medea
Merchant of Venice
Metamorphoses
The Metamorphosis
Middlemarch
A Midsummer Night's
  Dream
Moby Dick
A Modest Proposal and
  Other Satires
Moll Flanders
Mother Courage and Her
  Children
Mrs. Dalloway
Much Ado About
  Nothing
My Antonia
Mythology
Native Son
Nickel and Dimed: On
  (Not) Getting By in
  America
Night
Nine Stories
No Exit
Northanger Abbey
Notes from Underground
O Pioneers

For our full list of over 250 Study Guides, Quizzes,
Sample College Application Essays, Literature Essays and E-texts, visit:

**www.gradesaver.com**

# ClassicNotes

# GradeSaver™

*Getting you the grade since 1999*™

## Other ClassicNotes from GradeSaver™

The Odyssey
Oedipus Rex or Oedipus
   the King
Of Mice and Men
The Old Man and the Sea
Oliver Twist
On Liberty
On the Road
One Day in the Life of
   Ivan Denisovich
One Flew Over the
   Cuckoo's Nest
One Hundred Years of
   Solitude
Oroonoko
Oryx and Crake
Othello
Our Town
The Outsiders
Pale Fire
Pamela: Or Virtue
   Rewarded
Paradise Lost
A Passage to India
The Pearl
Percy Shelley: Poems
Perfume: The Story of a
   Murderer
Persepolis: The Story of
   a Childhood
Persuasion
Phaedra
Phaedrus
The Piano Lesson
The Picture of Dorian
   Gray

Poe's Poetry
Poe's Short Stories
Poems of W.B. Yeats:
   The Rose
Poems of W.B. Yeats:
   The Tower
The Poems of William
   Blake
The Poetry of Robert
   Frost
The Poisonwood Bible
Pope's Poems and Prose
Portrait of the Artist as a
   Young Man
Pride and Prejudice
The Prince
The Professor's House
Prometheus Bound
Pudd'nhead Wilson
Pygmalion
Rabbit, Run
A Raisin in the Sun
The Real Life of
   Sebastian Knight
Rebecca
The Red Badge of
   Courage
The Remains of the Day
The Republic
Rhinoceros
Richard II
Richard III
The Rime of the Ancient
   Mariner
Rip Van Winkle and
   Other Stories

The Road
Robinson Crusoe
Roll of Thunder, Hear
   My Cry
Romeo and Juliet
A Room of One's Own
A Room With a View
A Rose For Emily and
   Other Short Stories
Rosencrantz and
   Guildenstern Are
   Dead
Salome
The Scarlet Letter
The Scarlet Pimpernel
The Seagull
Season of Migration to
   the North
The Secret Life of Bees
Secret Sharer
Sense and Sensibility
A Separate Peace
Shakespeare's Sonnets
Shantaram
Short Stories of Ernest
   Hemingway
Siddhartha
Silas Marner
Sir Gawain and the
   Green Knight
Sister Carrie
Six Characters in Search
   of an Author
Slaughterhouse Five
Snow Falling on Cedars
The Social Contract

For our full list of over 250 Study Guides, Quizzes,
Sample College Application Essays, Literature Essays and E-texts, visit:

**www.gradesaver.com**

Made in the USA
Lexington, KY
15 January 2013